The Concert Book

James F. Hollan, CFRE

Bonus Books, Inc., Chicago

For My Darling Mary Lynn

You make every day a concert for me

ISBN: 1-56625-126-5
Library of Catalog Card Number: 99-61378

Bonus Books, Inc.
160 East Illinois Street
Chicago, IL 60611

First Edition

Printed in the United States of America

Table of Contents

Chapter 1
The Hard Travelers

The Hard Travelers were a few college friends who formed a folk group back in the 60s. They were actually quite good, even recorded a record before graduating and going their separate ways. Twenty-two years later they decided to get together for a one time only reunion concert. As with many men that age, it was a chance to recapture a bit of their youth. They had so much fun at the reunion that they elected to keep it going on a very part time basis, building quite a local following as they gained far more recognition in their revival stage than they had ever experienced in their original stage. They were all successful in their professional lives but they couldn't give up the sheer joy and exhilaration of performing live on stage, the magic elixir for all performers.

In 1988 they agreed to host a concert fund raiser for the Maryland Chapter of the Cystic Fibrosis Foundation. That first event was more a desire on the part of many good people to host a fun event while raising a few dollars for a worthy cause. There was no real plan for greatness, no sense of what this local event would become. They used a band shell at a local county park, gathered a bunch of musical "friends" and asked other volunteers to sell tickets, man the gates and help out with all the tasks from litter pick up to stage management. It was a mostly amateur event run by a bunch of volunteers who wanted to do something worthwhile while having a good time and they succeeded in that goal, raising $12,500 for the Maryland Chapter of The Cystic Fibrosis Foundation.

During that time The Travelers also made a new friend in the remarkably brave and charming CF poster child Debbie Klipsch. Debbie was a joy to be near, an always smiling motivator for everyone involved in the show, but she would lose her battle with CF that year and her death would help motivate everyone, including The Travelers, to do even more in their next concert.

The second annual concert was held once again at the band shell in the county park, provided free of charge by the county executive, but lessons learned from the first event led to a much better organized concert featuring The Hard Travelers and their musical friend Glenn Yarbrough, known for hits like "Baby The Rain Must Fall," as well as local Annapolis residents like jazz legend Charlie Byrd, who donated a few tunes. That second concert raised $51,000, an amount large enough to stir organizers into a careful reevaluation of the potential of this "fun" event. A year later the concert moved to a larger venue at The Merriweather Post Pavilion and the musical friend was Emmylou Harris who helped raise a new record that year of $88,000. In 1991 the magic $100,000 mark was crossed when The Hard Travelers featured Barbara Mandrell, raising $102,000.

For the fifth annual concert the Travelers moved to a new venue in Baltimore, Pier Six, overlooking the newly renovated Inner Harbor. They raised $121,500 with Lee Greenwood who brought everyone in the audience to their feet with his extraordinary rendition of "God Bless the USA." There wasn't a dry eye in the house that night, a moment to be repeated the following year when The Oak Ridge Boys were the featured musical "friends." Late in that show a number of our local CF kids joined The Oaks on stage as they performed "Thank God For Kids." It was an electrifying moment, one I remember clearly to this day, as we all realized how much more than a concert this was — it was about more than music, more than a good time. These kids and many others like them needed us and we were all, each and every person in that audience, in a position to help them. That 1993 Concert, the sixth annual, raised $201,000 only to be topped in 1993 when Kathy Mattea helped raise $323,000 in another sellout at The Pier.

The last big change in venue occurred in 1995 when The Hard Travelers moved the concert to The Baltimore Arena with 13,000 seats in order to accommodate Kenny Rogers as the special musical friend. Everything moved up in size as Kenny's concert raised just under $525,000. Think about it, over half a million dollars in one night! It wasn't a fluke either, as The Hard Travelers and musical friends Alabama would fill the Arena and set a new record of $706,000 the following year.

The Annual Hard Travelers and Friends Concert to benefit Cystic Fibrosis is now a solid fixture in the Baltimore-Washington area. Thanks to excellent coverage by local radio and television, the Cystic Fibrosis Foundation gets daily mention for several months prior to the event; more importantly, feature stories are developed not only about the concert itself but about how The Cystic Fibrosis Foundation benefits from the dollars raised. This annual concert is not only an extraordinary financial success, it is also a public relations gold mine. We will talk in more detail about this series of CF concerts throughout this book but let's switch, for the moment, to another example of a start up concert.

The Maryland School for the Blind, a private non-profit organization established in 1853, found itself in financial difficulty owing to budget cutbacks at the state level. Like many similar organizations, the school had vested little time in self promotion or high-level fund raising prior to this time and it had a low recognition level in the community at large. It was regularly confused with the Maryland School for the Deaf, a state agency, and, although it had no real enemies, it also had few, if any, friends at the state level. The school was all but invisible when it suddenly found itself in need of significant private and public sector support.

I was brought in to develop a number of new strategies for the school and went to work dealing with first-priority issues: beefing up the annual appeal, developing a pro-active public relations program, putting a basic lobbying network into place and moving a grant program into high gear; however, it was clear almost from the beginning that the school needed to find a positive way to call attention to itself as a way to develop potential support in the corporate sector as well as the public sector. As a professional fund raiser, I am intimately familiar with the generosity of people, still amazed at how much and how often people give for the purest of reasons. After years in the corporate sector, I'm also aware of the fact that fund raisers rarely convince corporations to give, instead, we convince the corporation to give to our cause. Like the old honey and vinegar example, I believe it's easier to get corporations involved when you give them something fun and satisfying in return for their donation. The more you bring to the table, the better your chance of success; moreover, you can help them decide to give even more in the years to come.

It would be nice if good deeds were enough to insure good public recognition, but that is not the case. The school's long history of good deeds and day after day good works were neither praised nor vilified. Like thousands of other great organizations, churches, temples, hospitals, half way houses and schools across the country, good work was not "newsworthy." If we wanted to get on the front pages we needed to kill someone or do something spectacular. Another story about the development of technology for kids with multiple disabilities would probably get two small paragraphs buried on page 14 of the E Section of the paper, the part only fund raisers and public relations people read. That is the reality of the news business.

The school needed funds immediately. It was in desperate need of better public recognition and it needed to develop friends in state government if it hoped to turn back a tide of slashed and frozen budgets from the state. Although it was a private, non-profit organization, 80% of the school's budget came through the State Department of Education. We had in place a moderately successful Annual Golf Tournament which netted about $15,000 after expenses and a 5K Race that was extraordinarily labor intensive, involved several hundred people and netted less than $5,000. We bagged the 5K race, left the golf tournament in place since it was almost self running and focused on establishing an annual concert since I was one of those odd folks who thought concerts were effective fundraising tools and I actually knew how they worked. Our formal goal was to develop an annual concert that would generate a net profit of at least $100,000 per year while developing new donors and a positive public image. We planned to arrive at that goal by the third concert with a short term goal of breaking even the first year and having a net profit of $50,000 in the second year. I was brought in during a time of crisis and blessed with a board of directors willing to take chances and give me the support needed to get this program off the ground. It took a lot of nerve on their part and I was committed to rewarding that trust.

Many of the details and examples in this book come directly from that first concert for the school since a start up is the most difficult concert to pull off. Our first Annual Concert would feature the incredible Ray Charles at the finest symphony hall in Baltimore. The

Governor agreed to be our honorary chairman, various state officials wrote glowing endorsements about our great work in the state, the local ABC television affiliate acted as our major media sponsor, supplying the evening news anchor as our MC and various newspapers and radio stations donated approximately $100,000 worth of advertising. To top it all off, we also raised just over $102,000 our first year out while making lots of new friends. It was a landmark event for the school as they moved up several levels on the scale of organizations gaining significant support from the corporate world. It also put the school on the radar of the political movers and shakers in the state. The Maryland School for the Blind had finally arrived as a major player in the world of Maryland corporate philanthropy.

I love special events in general and concerts in particular. I love the broad blank canvas that we get to fill with performers and patrons as we bring it all together in such a way that everyone is begging for more. I love the challenge, the art of it, but most importantly, I love the extraordinary benefit it can bring to an organization. Concerts raise far more than direct dollars for an organization. They are a tool for cultivating new board members, locating year-long corporate support and gaining positive public recognition, especially for organizations with limited visibility. Concerts are not for everyone but they are a dynamic and legitimate tool when used properly, a tool that should be in the tool box of every fund-raising executive.

I'm sorry to say that many of my peers in the professional fund-raising community have seen fit to write special events off as a waste of time. On more than one occasion I've noticed the condescending air of pity from otherwise knowledgeable fund raisers when I even suggest that special events are a powerful part of the fund-raising arsenal. You might think I'd blurted out something like "Golly, Gee, everybody! Let's have a big bake sale and use all the money to build a new hospital!" The fact is that too many of my fund-raising peers say "Concerts are not effective events for an organization," when they really should be saying, "I don't know how a concert works, I don't know how to use this tool."

Have you ever whacked your thumb with a hammer? Did you say something like "Damn hammer!" Did you perhaps use an even more colorful expression that transferred all blame for your mistake to the hammer? I once threw a hammer into the garbage after it attacked me. Several hours later I retrieved the hammer, but the experience had the desired effect and the hammer was much better behaved after we had established that I would no longer put up with its shortcomings and bad behavior. Are you getting the point here? Concerts are not right for everyone and they are not right for all situations, but they are a tool you should know how to use. Concert production, however, is generally learned by doing. It is a skill practiced far more by people coming from the performance end of the spectrum rather than the fund-raising end, and promoters have little interest in teaching the "secrets of their trade," as it is their livelihood. Other than a few pages in larger books about special events, no solid, practical, step-by-step guide on producing concerts has really addressed the needs of fund raisers as well as promoters. This book is meant to be just that, a practical manual outlining the entire process, warts and all. It is your chance to hang out with knowledgeable experts as they produce major concerts that move the mission of their organizations forward. We will walk through all the basic steps for a standard concert from the planning stage through the after-concert evaluations.

For this book I have arbitrarily defined major concerts as those that seat between 1,000 and 8,000 people. It's just a rule of thumb for the sake of organization and it allows me to have a separate chapter discussing the variations on these basic principles as they apply to small concerts, under 1,000 seats, and another chapter on the unique features of large concerts, over 8,000 seats. In addition, this book is packed with real examples of contracts, riders, planning forms, generic letters, programs, advertisements, seating charts and a myriad of other documents so that you can get the best possible sense of what is really involved. You can apply what you want to your own event, learn from my mistakes and build on my successes.

A one-time concert is fine and dandy, but it's like finding a gold nugget at the entrance to a gold mine. Some people will pick up the nugget and be on their way, delighted with their good fortune; others will take the nugget but also invest a little time in checking out the gold mine to see if there are more and bigger nuggets to be had. I'm of the latter school. A one-time concert is a singular event that can raise a lot of dollars now and leave you looking for new ways to raise dollars next year. An annual concert, on the other hand, becomes an ongoing source of funds as you build on your successes. You can develop a continuous pool of supporters. A single concert is a fund raiser whereas a series of concerts is "development." It is also the case that a properly run concert actually gets easier to plan and manage each year while generating even more income. I expect to make a profit the very first year out on a brand new concert; however, I estimate that it takes at least four years, and often more, until a new concert arrives at a maximum income level. I refer you back to the Cystic Fibrosis concert at the beginning of this chapter. Imagine if The Hard Travelers had quit after that first concert.

This book should give you a thorough and practical understanding of how concerts work and how they are put together. Work your way to the end and you will have a good working knowledge of this very powerful tool enabling you to decide if it is the appropriate tool for the job at hand. For those of you already producing concerts it can serve as a tool for comparison, a way to evaluate how and what you are doing; perhaps a source of new ideas or variations on old ones. For those of you being forced into a major concert by an over eager but under informed board or committee, this book may help you open their eyes. For those of you eager to learn I hope this book serves as the next best thing to actually being there. Now let's get on with the show.

Chapter 2
The Venue

Venue is a fancy way of saying, "The place you hold the concert," and the choice of venue is probably the most important factor in deciding what kind of concert you may present, since it will define the size of the concert. You can't hold big concerts in little halls and you don't want to hold little concerts in big halls. With a few subtle exceptions that we will discuss in the next chapter, a major act generally does not adjust their performance fee based on the size of the venue. If a major performer charges $50,000 for a one-night show and you have a venue with 500 seats then your cost per seat is $100 before you add in any other costs; however, if your venue has 5,000 seats your cost per seat is $10 before adding other costs — quite a difference when it comes to ticket pricing for exactly the same performance.

We will discuss ticket pricing in Chapter 4 and you will learn how to track the performance record of acts in Chapter 3. You will also learn how to find out the number of seats acts are currently selling for their shows and the average price per ticket for those shows. You will also see how many seats were available for sale in each of the venues and learn how many of those seats actually sold; consequently, you want to gather good data on what venue options are available in your area for comparative purposes. In a nutshell, if you find out performer X has played in a dozen different venues over the last month that have 3,000 seats or more, yet he has only sold an average of 1,500 tickets per show, you want either a different performer for a large hall or you want a hall that seats no more than 1,500. It may be a tad confusing now but it will become clear as we pull all the booking elements together.

A local venue search is fairly easy since you want to rent a hall and most halls want to rent to you. Get out the phone book and call all the choices in your area. Start with the biggest venues and ask them to send a rental packet, then work your way down the list of possible sites. If you are in New York or Los Angeles or any other big city you will have an amazingly diverse range of choices. If, on the otherhand, you are in East Nowhereville, you may have to reach way out to come up with any choice at all. I can't build any venues in your area but I can tell you how to use whatever is available. Remember that in Chapter 1 we set up an arbitrary rule of thumb for concerts that will seat between 1,000 and 8,000 people, so you don't need to focus on smaller or larger venues at present. I do, however, encourage you to look at all options in that seating range. You might be aware of shows at the Symphony Hall but unaware that a venue that normally does horse shows and rodeos also has a portable stage and set up for concerts. It may be a poor choice for some acts but perfect for others. Get the facts; they're free.

You will get a packet that should include seating charts, technical specifications, additional equipment and services available for rental as well as a list of costs for each of those services. Most packets are quite good and easy to understand as the venue needs and wants your business. Even the busiest concert hall is likely to have many days of the year when the hall is not in use and they have bills just like everyone else. Let's take a look at some examples from a typical packet. This one is from The Joseph Meyerhoff Symphony Hall, a wonderful venue that I've used on several occasions. We will refer back to these pages and fee schedules several times throughout this book as you see how we pick and choose those features that we want to add to our basic rental fee.

The cover letter from The Meyerhoff summarizes the key elements of this great facility. It has 2,465 seats and a number of other features including reception areas of different sizes, just perfect if you plan on having a before or after-concert reception.

The schedule of fees is fundamentally self explanatory but I would like to clarify a few points. There is a beautiful lobby for the general public and there is an additional lobby area with bars and room for catering that can easily be roped off for pre-concert

JOSEPH MEYERHOFF SYMPHONY HALL

<u>1996-97 FEE SCHEDULE</u>
This schedule subject to change at any time

<u>RENT</u>

<u>AUDITORIUM</u>
<u>Wednesday thru Sunday</u>
Evening	7:00–11:00 p.m.	3800.
Second Performance, same day		2800.
Matinee	12:00–5:00 p.m.	3300.
Morning	9:00 a.m.–12:30 p.m.	2800.
Full Day	9:00 a.m.–11:00 p.m.	7000.

<u>Monday & Tuesday</u>
Evening	7:00–11:00 p.m.	$ 3500.
Second Performance, same day		2500.
Matinee	12:00–5:00 p.m.	3200.
Morning	9:00 a.m.–12:30 p.m.	2700.
Full Day	9:00 a.m.–11:00 p.m.	6500.

<u>Additional Charges</u>
Delayed performance (beginning 15 minutes after advertised performance time) per 15 minutes	300.
•Set-up charge per 4 hour period	500.

<u>RECITAL HALL</u>
Any four hours	1000.

<u>LOBBY FOR RECEPTION</u> (with auditorium rental)
Up to 400 people	900.
400 to 1000 people	1600.
Over 1000 people	2500.

<u>GREEN ROOM</u> (for reception)
Any four hours	600.
Including outer hall	750.

<u>REHEARSAL ON STAGE</u>
Daytime – 4 hours – same day as event	500.
4:00 p.m. – Midnight – on day prior to event	800.
1 hour acoustical and/or sound check at no charge	

<u>HOUSE EQUIPMENT RENTALS</u>
Piano – 9 Ft. Steinway (1 tuning included)		450.
House Sound System		450.
Second Show		200.
Lectern and 1 Mike		50.
Monitor Speakers	Each	55.
House Lighting System Cove Lights		450.
Chorus Risers		60.
Production Office Phone (direct dial) Toll calls by credit card		.50
Ampex Professional Tape Recorders	Each	50.
Microphones	Each	15.

9/01/96

Joseph Meyerhoff Symphony Hall
1996–97 Fee Schedule

Xenon Super Trouper Spots	Each	145.
House Greenery		500.

BOX OFFICE SERVICES

Ticket Printing per set	175.
Additional show same day	75.
Box Office service (30 days) – cash sales only	735.
Additional show same day	365.
Box Office service (30 days) – charge and cash sales	1000.
Additional show same day	500.
Credit charges – 5%	At cost
Distribution only	500.
If Ticketmaster is used exclusively, Box Office charge	
Day of show	300.
2 shows same day	450.

IATSE PRODUCTION PERSONNEL

All stagehand calls are for a minimum of 4 hours, with a minimum of 4 men. An estimate must be obtained prior to signing of contract from Shop Steward, Ennis Seibert. Time and one-half applies on Sunday and doubletime on designated holidays and certain load-outs. The 1995–96 rate is $26.20 per man per hour plus fringes until March 1, 1996.

HOUSE MAINTENANCE PERSONNEL

Front of House Personnel (Manager, Head Usher,	
Ticket Takers, Ushers, Maintenance, Security)	1425.
Additional Concert Security, if needed	At cost
Nurse when requested	At cost
Front of House Personnel – Performances starting	
after 9:30 p.m. and on holidays	1650.

HOUSE SERVICES

Television and Film	1000.
Radio Broadcast	300.
Recording (commercial)	950.
Recording (non-commercial)	300.
Piano Tuning	90.

INSURANCE

Liability and Property damage/personal injury
   and Workers Comp –
Responsibility of presenter

MARYLAND STATE ADMISSIONS AND AMUSEMENT TAX

(Deducted at settlement if	
out-of-state presenter)	10% of ticket sales

CONCESSIONS

A charge of 10% (20% if J.M.S.H. staff sells) of gross sales will be made on sale of souvenir programs and/or recordings sold in J.M.S.H. The items sold must relate to show on stage and can be sold only in the lobby.

9/01/96

Joseph Meyerhoff Symphony Hall

1212 Cathedral Street, Baltimore, MD 21201   Phone: (410) 783-8100 Fax: (410) 783-8004

APPLICATION TO LEASE

Name of Licensee:_____

Contact: _____

Address:_____

Date Requested:_____
Alternate Dates: _____

Federal Identification No.:_____
Social Security No.: _____

Presenter is: _____ Corporation   State in which Incorporated _____
              _____ Partnership   Registered In _____
              _____ Individual
              _____ Other, please describe: _____

Names of: President _____
           Vice Presidents _____
           Financial Officer_____

Names of Partners: _____
_____
_____

Please list recent venues used:

Name of Venue   Contact   Telephone Number
_____   _____   _____
_____   _____   _____
_____   _____   _____

Please list name, address and telephone number of current bank.
_____
_____
_____
_____

Please list name and telephone number of an official at this bank as a reference.

_____

Describe your proposed event including names of artist, performers and speakers.

_____
_____
_____
_____
_____
_____

Please list two (2) venues the artist or performer has appeared in the past year.

_____
_____
_____
_____

Will this event be:
_____ For public sale   _____ By invitation only
_____ Free   _____ Other (please attach details)

Please attach any additional information pertinent to your presentation including audio/visual recordings, photographs, reviews, etc.

It is hereby agreed to by the person/organization (Licensee) requesting the use of the premises that no information or publicity of any nature relating to the proposed event may be announced or released in any manner until the standard agreement for lease is executed by JOSEPH MEYERHOFF SYMPHONY HALL and the Licensee and the deposit has been paid.

Furthermore, Licensee hereby represents that a full, accurate and complete disclosure of all information has been made and that the above statements and information are true and correct.

Signature: _____

Name: _____

Title: _____

Date: _____

Please return this request and all supporting materials to Barbara Kirstel, Hall Manager, 1212 Cathedral Street, Baltimore, MD 21201.

receptions. As you see on the chart the fee floats based on the number of people you plan to invite to the reception. The Green Room is a very elegant room for receptions with the main artist after the show. It holds up to 80 people and will be discussed later.

Each of the house equipment rental items are available if you need them. You might not need a piano but you might use the house sound system and chorus risers (those are platforms about eight inches high to give elevation to your band or chorus). You can also add to the equipment available through the hall by using other suppliers in the area. It is common to add additional sound and light for many of the shows I produce and we will discuss those aspects later in the book.

In addition to the house equipment you can rent box office services. They will print tickets, take phone orders for your show and collect payment. You can hire house personnel or use your own volunteers, the charges are all laid out for you with the exception of IATSE production costs. These are the charges for union personnel who operate the technical side of the production. We will discuss union personnel in Chapter 4 and Chapter 9 but it is not very difficult to get an estimate of the costs for personnel once you know the type of show you want to stage. The hall will have the address and phone number of the shop steward for the local branch of the union.

The last item on the fee schedule is often overlooked yet it can have significant benefit to your organization. The Hall as a policy charges a 10% commission on all promotional materials sold during the concert. When we get to the performers in the next chapter, you will see that they often want to sell CDs, tapes, T-shirts, etc. With a big group and a big audience it's easy to generate many thousands of dollars in sales. As the producer you should be getting your 10% of sales which can easily be another thousand or two in your pocket. If you provide volunteer sales help you might negotiate for 20%. We will discuss that in more detail later, but don't overlook the concession fees.

The technical specifications may sound like Greek to you and that's okay. They still sound like Greek to me, but they have meaning to the performer and you will compare this list of available equipment to the list of needed equipment provided by the performer. If something doesn't match you will call back and forth to see what must be available and what can be left out. All of this is done *before* any contracts are signed.

Since I use many sponsors for my concerts and I always have VIP tickets, the seating charts allow me to keep my VIPs happy by making them feel important, and seating them next to their peers is part of that process.

The last two pages from the Meyerhoff are your lease application. It's pretty self explanatory but you need to know that all reputable venues are nervous about leasing their facility to beginners. They have a reputation to maintain and they are not interested in having a poorly run event at their facility. It is likely that they can rent to someone else, or, if that is not the case, they will usually do without the fees in order to protect their reputation for quality performance. You are opening a dialogue with the hall manger that we will develop as we move through this book. At this stage, nothing is written in stone and most things are negotiable.

Don't try to understand everything yet as we still have a few pieces of the puzzle to put on the table. For the moment you have received some preliminary information about venues and you have seen a basic information packet from one of those venues. We will move forward now to the "sexiest" part of the process, locating and selecting the major performer for your major concert.

Chapter 3
The Performer

You have to take my word for it, but I'm actually a pretty classy guy, someone who moves smoothly and elegantly in different social circles; nevertheless, I often have this overwhelming desire to call all my friends and say "Holy Cow, you'll never guess who I just talked to! I just talked to Ray Charles! Really, Ray Charles! Can you believe it?"

I guess being suave means I don't actually do that, but I always want to. Even though I produce concerts, I've never really overcome the sense of unreality you get when you deal with people you grew up watching on TV or meet the singer of the songs you once fell in love to. There is a lot of work involved in planning a major concert but there are also some unique perks and this is one of them. We get to bathe in the glow of real honest to goodness stardom; have our fling, even if only by association, with the proverbial lights of Broadway.

The first step in choosing an act from the vast panoply of performers available is to select an act appropriate to your image. By that I mean it is foolhardy to hire some hot new group with a name like Putrid Death Wish if you hope to develop an image of warm and fuzzy responsibility. Acts have a personality that transcends the performance so that the sponsoring organization is actually washed in the image of the performer. There are family type performers, raunchy performers, performers that attract the young or the old as well as cross-generational performers. There are performers who are on the way up and performers on the way down. Different acts appeal to different audiences, some with very narrow appeal, others with extraordinarily broad appeal.

As an example, let me describe a catastrophe for a non-profit organization that provides immediate shelter to battered women and their children. They hired a legendary rock and roll/blues performer to give a benefit concert. The act was so well known and respected that the concert sold out. Shortly before the show the performer pointed out that they had changed the act and would have two parts requiring a costume change in the middle. In order to bridge the 20-minute gap the star had asked their son to perform with his new "rap" act. In reality, the star was trying to give their kid a break into the business, so they had created this "opportunity" during their concert schedule. Although the promoters had a contract in hand that said the performer would give one continuous 90-minute performance, they didn't want to upset the star so they agreed. The performer gave the first half of the performance, which left the audience begging for more, and then they introduced their son and his new act.

The son's act was vulgar and sexist. It encouraged the abuse of "bitches" among other things and so offended the audience that hundreds of people got to their feet and left, many from the VIP and sponsor-reserved sections. It was absolutely awful and totally counter productive to the goals and mission of the organization. The promoters gave up control of the show and ended up with a public relations nightmare. They could not have had a more inappropriate act on stage.

On the other side of the spectrum, it so happens that the first major concert we presented for The Maryland School for the Blind featured the one and only Ray Charles. The tie-in was so perfect at so many levels that I won't bore you with the repetition; however, he was such a perfect fit that we postponed our first concert for one year in order to open with Ray. When I first proposed a major concert to our board of directors they were justifiably nervous, but the suggestion that we open with someone like Ray Charles captured everyone's attention, so much so that one of the board members stood and pledged his firm as a sponsor for a Ray Charles concert and the board went ahead and approved a budget for a Ray Charles concert. I went into the meeting suggesting someone *like* Ray Charles and came out of the meeting with directions to *have* Ray

Charles. Talk about painting yourself into a corner! Of course the thing that happened is everyone realized he was the perfect fit for our image. He was a cross generational draw, a true musical legend and the very epitome of someone rising above their disability. He was almost self defining as the perfect act for a blind school.

I'm not in any way suggesting that you must have a performer with a disability if your organization provides services for people with disabilities. I'm saying that the act you choose must do more than fill seats. They must be appropriate to the kind of organization you are, since ultimately you are creating a fund raiser *and* an image enhancer.

You also need to have some sense of the audience you are approaching as you select an act. By audience I mean not only the actual people who sit through the concert but the sponsors you hope to involve in your show. It's not your goal to be hip or to get the most current hot performer. It's not your goal to be popular with the young staff at your organization. It's not your goal to get an act that satisfies the taste of the chairman of the board who still thinks that nothing beats barber shop for real music. It's your goal to find an act that will fill your venue and enhance the positive public image of your organization.

So where do you start? The fact is that ignorance is sometimes bliss, so you might as well start with a brainstorming session that tosses up names of acts that you would like to have. Without any coaching you'll probably get a sense of the kind of acts that seem appropriate to the kind of image you're hoping to project. Let the names flow as you create a list of potential performers. It's a list that will later help you define the type of act you are searching for and it may also help an agent locate a similar but more affordable act that you didn't think about the first time around.

It is most helpful to have a list of performers as a reference point or source of names. These lists are available through several trade publications. The major resource I use to track performers and locate the agents representing various talent is *Pollstar*. They have a website at http://www.pollstar.com and they can be reached by more traditional means at 4697 W. Jacquelyn Ave., Fresno, CA 93722. Phone (559) 271-7900 or Fax (559) 271-7979. *Pollstar* is a weekly publication that lists major artists, where they are playing, how many seats they've sold, and average ticket prices, and that ranks that week's performance by income. They also run special agency roster issues that list every major talent agency and the performers they represent. Since there are many thousands of performers, they additionally run an alphabetical list of performers in the back of this issue with a cross index to the talent agency that represents them. If you wanted, for example, to find out what it takes to hire blues legend, B.B. King, you would flip to the back of the book, look him up in the alphabetical list and find that he is represented by Associated Booking Corporation. You would then look Associated Booking Corporation up in the front of the book and get the address and phone number. You would also see a list of the other performers represented by Associated Booking. You can pick up the phone and call to find out what it would cost to get Mr. King to come and play for your organization. It's that easy; however, I recommend that you read the next few chapters before placing any calls since you might not understand some of the terms used by the agency.

The only down side to *Pollstar* is that an annual subscription costs $315, which is a bit steep for those just looking for one act a year. I generally find a few old copies at one of the venues I'm considering or I ask some of the other professionals in the area if they have a slightly out of date copy. It is such a powerful tool when you are trying to lock down performers and figure out who might work in your area that I recommend you subscribe if you can afford it. The price of an act is ultimately decided by the number of seats they can sell in general and the market is constantly shifting. You need to know what kind of draw an act has currently and *Pollstar* is the source of that information. I've attached a page from a June 1998 issue of *Pollstar*. On page 22 I've zoomed in on one section of this page so that we can better examine the detail given.

According to this chart Michael Flatley's "Lord of the Dance" concert played three different shows at the Bellville Velladrome in South Africa. The dates were May 19, 20 and 21. The Velladrome has 5,856 seats and all three shows sold out (100% of seats sold). The ticket price range went from $20 to $70. Since these shows were in South Africa, prices were converted from the local currency, the Rand. These three shows brought in $872,770.

Eric Clapton played the America West Arena in Phoenix, Arizona on May 25. His opening act was DC 6. The venue has 13,347 seats and Eric sold 100% of them. Ticket prices went from $34.75 to $80.10. The total sales were $771,560 for that night.

BOXOFFICE SUMMARY

Date	Artist / Facility/Promoter	Support	Tickets Sold / Capacity	Gross
06/13/98 06/14/98 2 Shows	"Tibetan Freedom Concert" / RFK Stadium / Washington, DC / Cellar Door Concerts / Milarepa	Red Hot Chili Peppers / Dave Matthews Band / REM / Herbie Hancock/Live/Pearl Jam / Blues Traveler/Wallflowers	118,681 / 59,341 / 100% / 27.50-60.00	3,393,613
05/26/98 05/27-31 7 Shows	Michael Flatley's "Lord Of The Dance" / MTN Sundome / Johannesburg, SOUTH AFRICA / Big Concerts / Attie van Wyk		63,294 / 9,042 / 100% / 20.00-70.00	2,739,302 Rand (14,134,803)
06/05/98 06/06-14 15 Shows	"Nickelodeon Presents: Rugrats Live" / Rosemont Theatre / Rosemont, IL / The Entertainment Group		46,043 / 3,400 / 90% / 17.50-29.50	1,192,240
05/19/98 05/20-21 3 Shows	Michael Flatley's "Lord Of The Dance" / Bellville Velladrome / Cape Town, SOUTH AFRICA / Big Concerts / Attie van Wyk		17,568 / 5,856 / 100% / 20.00-70.00	872,770 Rand (4,593,525)
05/25/98	Eric Clapton / America West Arena / Phoenix, AZ / Evening Star Productions	DC 6	13,347 / 13,347 / 100% / 34.75-80.10	771,560
05/29/98	Eric Clapton / Arrowhead Pond of Anaheim / Anaheim, CA / Nederlander Concerts	DC6	12,770 / 12,770 / 100% / 35.00-75.00	690,835
05/17/98	Dave Matthews Band / Shoreline Amphitheatre / Mountain View, CA / Bill Graham Presents	Taj Mahal	22,030 / 22,030 / 100% / 30.00	660,900
06/12/98 06/13/98 2 Shows	Yanni / Lakewood Amphitheatre / Atlanta, GA / Cascade Concerts / Danny O'Donovan		10,162 / 6,430 / 79% / 55.00-80.00	632,334
05/24/98 05/25/98 2 Shows	Dave Matthews Band / Red Rocks Amphitheatre / Denver, CO / Bill Graham Presents / Chuck Morris Presents	Taj Mahal (5/24) / Poi Dog Pondering (5/25)	18,670 / 9,335 / 100% / 30.00	562,800
06/12/98	Page / Plant / Target Center / Minneapolis, MN / Jam Productions	Lili Haydn	13,442 / 13,442 / 100% / 30.00-65.00	507,000
05/23/98 05/24/98 2 Shows	Michael Flatley's "Lord Of The Dance" / Superbowl / Sun City, SOUTH AFRICA / Big Concerts / Attie van Wyk		10,088 / 5,044 / 100% / 20.00-70.00	490,365 Rand (2,580,866)
06/09/98	Shania Twain / General Motors Place / Vancouver, BC, CANADA / Universal Concerts Canada	Leahy	17,845 / 17,845 / 100% / 37.50-49.50	487,282 Canadian (696,117)
06/13/98 06/14/98 2 Shows	James Taylor / Cynthia Woods Mitchell Pavilion / The Woodlands, TX / Pace Concerts		22,142 / 12,814 / 86% / 15.00-35.00	482,150
06/09/98	Page / Plant / Market Square Arena / Indianapolis, IN / Sunshine Promotions	Lili Haydn	11,474 / 18,096 / 63% / 32.50-47.50	457,325
05/25/98 05/26/98 2 Shows	Yes / Auditorio Nacional / Mexico City, MEXICO / O.C.E.S.A. Presents / Cie Presents		18,045 / 9,832 / 92% / 110.00-450.00	439,898 Pesos (3,999,070)
06/07/98	Page / Plant / Kiel Center / St. Louis, MO / Contemporary Productions	Lili Haydn	11,545 / 12,995 / 89% / 29.00-40.00	438,840
06/10/98	Page / Plant / Bradley Center / Milwaukee, WI / Cellar Door Concerts	Lili Haydn	10,471 / 18,630 / 56% / 29.50-46.00	415,178
05/23/98 05/24/98 2 Shows	"Mountain Aire" / Calaveras County Fair / Angels Camp, CA / Bill Graham Presents	Ben Harper / Leftover Salmon / Charlie Hunter / Last Caravan / Clan / Widespread Panic / moe. / Greyboy Allstars/Galactic	12,451 / 7,500 / 83% / 29.50-55.00	351,620
06/13/98	Stevie Nicks / P.N.C. Bank Arts Center / Holmdel, NJ / Pace Concerts / Delsener/Slater Enterprises	Boz Scaggs	9,437 / 17,076 / 55% / 24.00-60.00	328,672
06/14/98	Lynyrd Skynyrd / Coca-Cola Star Lake Amphitheatre / Burgettstown, PA / DiCesare-Engler Productions	Peter Frampton / Freddy Jones Band	21,702 / 22,593 / 96% / 15.00-35.00	328,602
06/01/98	Page / Plant / Birmingham-Jefferson Coliseum / Birmingham, AL / New Era Promotions		9,939 / 11,904 / 83% / 29.50-40.00	320,930
05/01/98	Alan Jackson / Edmonton Coliseum / Edmonton, ALB, CANADA / Universal Concerts Canada	Deana Carter	11,553 / 13,000 / 89% / 37.75	305,288 Canadian (436,125)
06/09/98	Stevie Nicks / Coca-Cola Star Lake Amphitheatre / Burgettstown, PA / Pace Concerts / DiCesare-Engler Productions	Boz Scaggs	15,111 / 22,593 / 67% / 20.50-50.00	285,845
05/30/98	Boyz II Men / Rose Garden Arena / Portland, OR / Bill Graham Presents	Destiny's Child / Uncle Sam	8,068 / 8,068 / 100% / 30.00-37.50	284,904
06/12/98	The Moody Blues / P.N.C. Bank Arts Center / Holmdel, NJ / Pace Concerts / Delsener/Slater Enterprises		9,371 / 17,076 / 55% / 20.00-49.50	280,119
06/08/98	Yanni / Hartford Civic Center Coliseum / Hartford, CT / Cascade Concerts / Danny O'Donovan		5,412 / 8,443 / 64% / 39.50-65.00	274,393
06/10/98	Yanni / Charlotte Coliseum / Charlotte, NC / Cascade Concerts / Danny O'Donovan		6,447 / 8,122 / 79% / 35.00-50.00	263,870
06/13/98	"Kings Of Comedy" / Market Square Arena / Indianapolis, IN / Southeast Concerts/Contemporary Prod.	Steve Harvey / Bernie Mac / Cedric The Entertainer / Guy Torry	6,896 / 10,000 / 69% / 35.00-50.00	260,135
06/14/98	Yanni / The Crown / Cincinnati, OH / Cascade Concerts / Danny O'Donovan		6,293 / 8,981 / 70% / 38.50-56.00	255,871
06/13/98	Deep Purple "Monsters Of Rock" / Palastampa / Torino, ITALY / Barley Arts Promotions	Dream Theater / Joe Satriani / MSG / Saxon / Overkill / Jon Roth / Hammerfall	8,800 / 9,000 / 98% / 50,000	248,996 Lira (440,000,000)
06/13/98	Michael Bolton / Wynonna / Coca-Cola Star Lake Amphitheatre / Burgettstown, PA / Pace Concerts / DiCesare-Engler Productions		16,706 / 22,593 / 74% / 16.00-55.00	227,164
06/05/98 06/06/98 2 Shows	"Lord Of The Dance" / Sioux Falls Arena / Sioux Falls, SD / Contemporary Productions	John Carey / Arelenn Boyle / Clan Nolan / Gillian Norris	4,993 / 4,900 / 51% / 35.00-45.00	223,435
05/02/98	Alan Jackson / Canadian Airlines Saddledome / Calgary, ALB, CANADA / Universal Concerts Canada	Deana Carter	8,426 / 12,500 / 67% / 37.50	221,183 Canadian (315,975)
06/14/98 2 Shows	Vince Gill / Palace Theatre At Myrtle Beach / Myrtle Beach, SC / (In-House Promotion)		5,200 / 2,600 / 100% / 39.25-43.55	209,542
06/04/98	"Lord Of The Dance" / Fargodome / Fargo, ND / Contemporary Productions	John Carey / Areleen Boyle / Clan Nolan / Gillian Norris	5,179 / 9,330 / 56% / 25.00-45.00	205,625
06/12/98	Lynyrd Skynyrd / Deer Creek Music Center / Noblesville, IN / Sunshine Promotions	Peter Frampton / Freddy Jones Band	15,578 / 20,000 / 78% / 10.00-25.50	205,471
06/06/98	Tony Bennett / Star Plaza Theatre / Merrillville, IN / Star Productions		3,400 / 3,400 / 100% / 60.00	204,000
06/12/98	"Kings Of Comedy" / Wisconsin Center Arena / Milwaukee, WI / Southeast Concerts/Contemporary Prod.	Steve Harvey / Bernie Mac / Cedric The Entertainer / Guy Torry	4,839 / 8,000 / 60% / 40.00-52.00	202,673
06/09/98	Boyz II Men / Sandstone Amphitheatre / Bonner Springs, KS / Contemporary Productions	K-Ci & JoJo / Next	7,958 / 18,000 / 44% / 15.00-39.50	202,590

Fax your box office results.

It's quick, accurate and simple.

Fax us at **209 271.7979**

or call us between 8 am and 5 pm.

Pacific Time: **800 344.7383**

In California Call: **209 271-7900**

"Used by permission of Pollstar."

05/19/98	**Michael Flatley's "Lord Of The Dance"**		**17,568**	**872,770**
05/20-21	Bellville Velladrome		5,856	
	Cape Town, SOUTH AFRICA		100%	Rand
3 Shows	Big Concerts / Attie van Wyk		20.00-70.00	(4,593,525)
05/25/98	**Eric Clapton**	DC 6	**13,347**	**771,560**
	America West Arena		13,347	
	Phoenix, AZ		100%	
	Evening Star Productions		34.75-80.10	
05/29/98	**Eric Clapton**	DC6	**12,770**	**690,835**
	Arrowhead Pond Of Anaheim		12,770	
	Anaheim, CA		100%	
	Nederlander Concerts		35.00-75.00	
05/17/98	**Dave Matthews Band**	Taj Mahal	**22,030**	**660,900**
	Shoreline Amphitheatre		22,030	
	Mountain View, CA		100%	
	Bill Graham Presents		30.00	

Four nights later Eric Clapton played at Arrowhead Pond in Anaheim, California and he had another sell out. This time the venue was a bit smaller at 12,770 seats and tickets were a tad cheaper, running $35 to $75 each. Total sales were $690,835 for that night.

Notice that the acts are rated weekly by gross dollars and The Dave Matthews Band came in next with a show at the Shoreline Amphitheatre in Mountain View, California. Tickets were $30 and all 22,030 sold. The opening act was Taj Mahal.

This list moves right on down through smaller and smaller venues. The bottom of the list this week was an act in Vancouver, British Columbia. A total of 37 tickets were sold for a hall that seats 500. Ticket prices were $7 and $8. The total take for the evening was $200 U.S. We will leave the act nameless for this book, but you can see how extraordinarily helpful this information is when you want to see how acts are doing out on the road. Do you see what I mean when I say that *Pollstar* is a very powerful tool?

I know I'm moving quickly here, but I want you to get a complete walk through the entire process before we revisit key points. You've now learned how and where to find out the performance statistics of acts you are interested in and you've learned how to locate their agents. I should point out that this skill alone is used by many booking agents who do little more than act as a go between for agencies and organizations who wish to book a major act. They rarely gain any benefit for the sponsoring organization and they charge a fee for their services. In far too many cases they make thousands of dollars for placing a few calls that you could place yourself. Some booking agents offer a useful and valuable range of services but many do not. Buyer Beware!

The agency, on the other hand, is the official representative of the act, and for most major acts, the agency will have many agents working for them. When you call to inquire about an act, the receptionist at the agency will generally ask where you are planning to present your concert and you will often be connected with an agent representing your geographic area. An agent can give you information about *all* the acts his agency represents and he is a wellspring of information. Although he or she works for the performer, it is their goal to have a successful performance all around. In general, they don't like to work with amateurs and beginners, but they do, so be professional and courteous in your dealings with them and you will learn a lot. Don't be snowballed either. If you don't understand something, ask again for an explanation.

It is important that you understand a few key elements before talking with an agent. The vast majority of acts have *on tour* and *off tour* rates. In general, artists go out on the road for many months at a time and travel with their main show, trying to hook up as many continuous dates in as many contiguous places as possible. It is a difficult process but generally to everyone's benefit if the performer can be booked during this road process. The *off tour* rate for a performer is often two or three times their *on tour* rate. When asking for the cost of a performer make sure you get both rates. Also make sure that you understand what you get for the rate.

For example, the Ray Charles *on tour* rate in the summer of 1997 was $40,000 for a show that included his stage band and his back up singers the Rayletts. If you wanted to book Ray *off tour* the price was $50,000; however, that was only for Ray and his key staff. We would additionally have to hire a full orchestra for a show and additionally pay for a full rehearsal, pay an extra fee to the Hall for rehearsal time, and provide first-class air transportation, ground transportation and hotel accommodations for Ray and his staff. The estimated cost for this show *off tour*, with a pick up orchestra came out at approximately $75,000, almost twice as much as the on tour rate.

After the cost you must always ask for the riders. Riders are all the extra things that are in the contract that you *must* do. Most are common sense requests from performers who are in a different town every night. They are stuck in their dressing room for hours on end and they don't want your Aunt Bertha's special Muskrat Surprise for dinner along with a bottle of your home brewed beer. It is common to see requests for specific food and drink to be provided before show time. The requests are usually sensible, asking for bottled water, ice, soda, tea or coffee, a cheese tray, sandwiches or fruit. Some are more elaborate and some, like the famous M&M candies with all the green ones removed, are ridiculous.

Riders will often include lodging, air fare, ground transportation and meals; consequently, they can add significant dollars to your performer's cost. Two key points to remember about riders is that some items, for example hotel rooms and suites, can be donated as gifts in kind by local hotels in return for recognition as a sponsor. More importantly, remember that most riders are negotiable. Limousines for pick up at the airport can often be negotiated to vans, suites can often be negotiated to doubles and requests for open-ended first-class airfare can often be negotiated to a flat fee towards transportation. In fact, I've been very successful with just saying "No" to most riders dealing with transportation.

I can't tell you the number of people I know who've booked an act through an agency or middle man at a fixed rate, never inquired about the riders, then blithely signed the contract, committing themselves to thousands of dollars in additional costs. Remember the example of Ray Charles above and the impact that riders can have on final cost for the performer. You must ask what the riders are right up front. It saves everyone time and energy.

Now that you understand the difference between off tour and on tour rates and you have a sense as to how riders can impact your cost, you are ready to talk to an agent. Let's say that you've selected several potential acts and you find that three are represented by the same agency. You just want to get an idea as to cost and availability, so you place a tentative call to the agency. You should expect a conversation that goes something like this after getting through a receptionist or two:

AGENT: "This is Joe Agent, how can I help you?"
YOU: "I'm the Director of Development at The Meaningful Organization and we are planning the first in what we hope to be an annual series of concerts as a fund raiser for our organization. I'm calling to find out how much it would cost to book some of your acts."

AGENT: "Do you have a venue yet?"

YOU: " Yes, I've had some preliminary conversations with the Meyerhoff Symphony Hall here in Baltimore."

AGENT: "How many seats?"

YOU: "About 2,400 for the show."

AGENT: "Okay, who are you interested in?"

YOU: "Well our first choice would be Tony Bennett, but I don't really have any idea what he would cost for an evening."

AGENT: "Tony Bennett on tour is going to cost you $125,000."

YOU: "Oh! I'm afraid that's more than we were planning to spend."

AGENT: "What is your budget?"

YOU: "Well, for the performer we were trying to stay under $40,000."

AGENT: "Let me see." (You hear him rustling through the pages of a notebook.)

"How about someone like Jose Feliciano? He puts on an excellent show and it would only cost you $35,000."

YOU: "No, I'm looking for someone with a broader base. How much is someone like Stevie Wonder?"

AGENT: "He would cost somewhere between $150,000 and $200,000."

YOU: "Oh."

AGENT: "How about Willie Nelson? You can book him on tour for $40,000."

YOU: "Gee, I hadn't thought of him, but he sure would be a possibility."

AGENT: "What dates are you looking for?"

YOU: "We want to hold the concert next June. We have a few possible open dates available at The Meyerhoff, June 19 or 20 and June 26 or 27."

AGENT: "Let me see." (You hear more rustling of pages as he checks another book.) "No, I'm sorry, he'll be on tour in Europe then. Let me look a little further." (More rustling of pages.) "How about The Smothers Brothers and The Kingston Trio? They are available on June 19 and 20. I can deliver them at a package price of $40,000."

YOU: "Wow! I never thought of them but that's a real possibility. Are there any riders with that?"

AGENT: "They need first-class air fare for 10 people, five suites and five king rooms and limousines for ground transportation."

YOU: "Our budget pushes up close to $40,000 as is. I think we can cover the rooms and ground transportation if vans are okay, but we wouldn't be able to do the air fare on top of everything."
AGENT: "I can probably get them to waive the air fare."
YOU: "Okay, they are a real possibility. Can you send me a contract to review?"
AGENT: "Sure, send me a written request and I'll put one in the mail to you."

Perhaps a little simple minded, but that is the gist of it. You more than likely will make several calls to several agents getting ranges of prices for acts and availability. Some will have very elaborate promotional kits they will send along with reviews, photos, tapes and even video collections of the performer that you can pop in your VCR while reading about the act. You are committed to nothing yet. You're just narrowing down the possibilities as you try to get the right act in the right place at the right time for the right price.

Once again, let's move rapidly forward so that you can see the entire process once through. Let's assume you decided on your performer, the dates work and you tell the agent to go ahead and send the contract for review. Several days later a document will arrive similar to the one beginning on the following page. Let's take a look at it and see what is and what is not written in stone. It may seem formidable at first, but is not all that complex if you take your time and walk through it.

I know the contract may look mind boggling but just take a breath or two and we will walk through the high points. The vast majority of material is generic boiler plate from standard contracts and another big hunk is a list of technical specifications that you will review with your stage manager or shop steward or the concert hall manager. There are a number of key points, however, that require your special attention. In particular, you want to make sure that those things you agreed to over the phone are in the contract. I have never once seen a contract for a performer that did not need some corrections.

The cover sheet on this contract is a summary of the key points. The talent agency is the William Morris Agency, the people I spoke to on the phone. The "producer" is Knave Productions. They represent the "artist," The Smothers Brothers, directly, and as with

WILLIAM MORRIS AGENCY, INC. / XXXX
Talent and Literary Agency
151 El Camino Drive • Beverly Hills • CA • 90212
Telephone 310-859-4000   Facsimile 310-859-4440

RIDER ATTACHED HERETO HEREBY MADE A PART OF THIS CONTRACT

Agreement made JAN 12 98 between Knave Productions, Inc. (hereinafter referred to as "PRODUCER") furnishing the services of THE SMOTHERS BROTHERS (hereinafter referred to as "ARTIST") and MARYLAND SCHOOL FOR THE BLIND/David Evans (hereinafter referred to as "PURCHASER")

It is mutually agreed between the parties as follows:

The PURCHASER hereby engages the PRODUCER and the PRODUCER hereby agrees to furnish the entertainment presentation hereinafter described, upon all the terms and conditions herein set forth, including those on the reverse side hereof entitled "Additional Terms and Conditions."

1. Place of Engagement: Meyerhoff Symphony Hall
                                         1212 Cathedral Street
                                         Baltimore, Maryland

         Scaling   0 @ $ 0.00
         Capacity: 0   Gross Potential: $0
                                        Tax: 0.00000
                         Net Potential: $0 (Not to exceed)
                                         Benefit concert for the
                                         Maryland School for the Blind

2. DATE(S) OF ENGAGEMENT: Sun JUN 28 98 -

     a. Number of Shows: 1
     b. Time of Show(s):   7:00 PM
     c. Length of Each Show: 60 minutes

3. BILLING: (In all forms of advertising)

     Artist shall receive 100% Sole Headline Billing

4. FULL PRICE AGREED UPON:

     $25,000 (Twenty Five Thousand) FLAT GUARANTEE
     Purchaser to provide and pay for: sound and lights, backline equipment and internal ground transportation per Artist rider, plus 2 one-bedroom suites and 3 king single hotel rooms for the nights of June 27 & 28, 1998.
     The Kingston Trio to perform prior to The Smothers Brothers.
     Purchaser requests that The Smothers Brothers be available prior to the show for press purposes and 30 mintues after for a Meet & Greet with major donors and local celebrities.
     Purchaser shall provide and pay for all terms and conditions contained in Artist rider attached hereto.
     All Accommodation and Travel arrangements are subject to PRODUCER's prior approval.

5. All payments shall be paid by PURCHASER in US funds by CERTIFIED or CASHIER'S CHECK, or CASH as follows:

     a. $12,500 shall be paid to and in the name of PRODUCER's agent, William Morris Agency not later than MAY 28 98

ADDITIONAL TERMS AND CONDITIONS CONTINUED ON REVERSED SIDE.

Additional Terms and Conditions

b. The balance in the amount of $12,500
shall be paid to and in the name of the PRODUCER: Knave Productions Inc. f/s/o
THE SMOTHERS BROTHERS not later than immediately prior to the first performance.

c. Earned percentages, overages and/or bonuses, if applicable, are to be paid to PRODUCER by CASH ONLY immediately following the last show.

d. In the event the FULL PRICE AGREED UPON to be paid by PURCHASER DOES NOT include percentages or overages, and the actual gross box office receipts from the engagement exceed the gross potential as stated in Paragraph 1, hereinabove, such amounts shall be paid in full to PRODUCER in CASH ONLY, immediately following the last performance.

6. PURCHASER shall first apply any and all receipts derived from the entertainment presentation to the payments required hereunder. All payments shall be made in full without any deductions whatsoever. PURCHASER will advise PRODUCER, or PRODUCER's agent, promptly upon request of the admissions prices for the entertainment presentation.

7. In the event the payment to PRODUCER shall be based in whole or in part on receipts of the performance(s) hereunder, PURCHASER agrees to deliver to PRODUCER a certified statement of the gross receipts of each performance within two (2) hours following such performance. In the further event that the payment of PRODUCER's share of said performance(s) receipts is based in whole or in part upon expenses related to the engagement, PURCHASER shall verify by paid receipts, cancelled checks or similar documents all such expenses or they shall not be included as an expense of the engagement. PRODUCER shall have the right to have a representative present in the box office at all times and such representative shall have access to box office records of PURCHASER relating to gross receipts of this engagement only.

8. PURCHASER agrees to furnish and pay for at its own expense (a) on the date and at the time of the performance(s) above-mentioned all that is necessary for the proper presentation of the entertainment presentation, including without limitation a suitable theatre, hall or auditorium, well-heated, ventilated, lighted, clean and in good order, stage curtains, properly tuned grand piano(s) and public address system in perfect working condition including microphone(s) in number and quality required by PRODUCER, dressing rooms, all necessary electricians and stage hands, all lights, tickets, house programs, all licenses (including musical performing rights licenses), special police, ushers, ticket sellers, ticket takers, appropriate and sufficient advertising in the principal newspapers, (b) all music royalties in connection with PRODUCER's use of music, and in addition, the costs of any musicians (including Contractor) other than those furnished by PRODUCER as part of PRODUCER's regular company, (c) all amusement taxes, (d) if PRODUCER so requires, all necessary facilities, electricians, stage hands and other personnel for lighting and dress rehearsals, and (e) all other items and personnel (including but not limited to any and all personnel, including musicians, as may be required by any national or local union(s)) required for the proper presentation of the entertainment presentation hereunder, and any rehearsals therefor, except for those items and personnel which PRODUCER herein specifically agrees to furnish. PRODUCER shall have the right to name the local music contractor and to approve the musicians hired locally.

9. In the event of sickness or of accident to ARTIST, or if a performance is prevented, rendered impossible or infeasible by any act or regulation of any public authority or bureau, civil tumult, strike, epidemic, interruption in or delay of transportation services, war conditions or emergencies or any other similar or dissimilar cause beyond the control of PRODUCER, it is understood and agreed that there shall be no claim for damages by PURCHASER and PRODUCER's obligations as to such performances shall be deemed waived. In the event of such non-performance for any of the reasons stated in

this paragraph, if ARTIST is ready, willing and able to perform, PURCHASER shall pay the full compensation hereunder, otherwise, the monies (if any) advanced to PRODUC-ER hereunder, shall be returned on a pro-rata basis.

10. Inclement weather rendering performance impossible, infeasible or unsafe shall not be deemed a force majeure event and payment of the agreed upon compensation shall be made notwithstanding. If PURCHASER and PRODUCER disagree as to whether rendition of performance(s) is impossible, not feasible or unsafe because of inclement weather, PRODUCER's determination as to performance shall prevail.

11. In the event PURCHASER refuses or neglects to provide any of the items or to perform any of its obligations herein stated, and/or fails to make any of the payments as provided herein, PRODUCER shall have the right to refuse to perform this contract, shall retain any amounts theretofore paid to PRODUCER by PURCHASER, and PUR-CHASER shall remain liable to PRODUCER for the agreed price herein set forth. In addition, if, on or before the date of any scheduled performance, PURCHASER has failed, neglected, or refused to perform any contract with any other performer for any other engagement, or if the financial standing or credit of PURCHASER has been impaired or is in PRODUCER's opinion unsatisfactory, PRODUCER shall have the right to demand the payment of the guaranteed compensation forthwith. If PURCHASER fails or refuses to make such payment forthwith, PRODUCER shall have the right to cancel this engagement by notice to PURCHASER to that effect, and to retain any amounts theretofore pait to PRODUCER by PURCHASER and PURCHASER shall remain liable to PRODUCER for the agreed price herein set forth.

12. The entertainment presentation to be furnished by PRODUCER hereunder shall receive billing in such order, form, size and prominence as directed by PRODUCER in all advertising and publicity issued by or under the control of the PURCHASER. ARTIST's name or likeness may not be used as an endorsement or indication of use of any product or service nor in connection with any corporate sponsorship or tie-up, commercial tie-up or merchandising without PRODUCER's prior written consent.

13. PURCHASER shall not itself, nor shall it permit others to record, broadcast or televise, photograph or otherwise reproduce the visual and/or audio performances hereunder, or any part thereof.

14. PRODUCER shall have the exclusive right to sell souvenir programs, ballet books, photographs, records and any and all types of merchandise including, but not limited to, articles of clothing (i.e., T-shirts, hats, etc.), posters, stickers, etc., on the premises of the place(s) of performance without any participation in the proceeds by PURCHASER subject, however, to concessionaire's requirements, if any.

15. Unless stipulated to the contrary in writing, PURCHASER agrees that PRODUCER may cancel the engagement hereunder without liability by giving the PURCHASER notice thereof at least thirty (30) days prior to the commencement date of the engagement hereunder. PRODUCER shall also have the right to terminate this agreement without liability in the event PURCHASER fails to sign and return this Contract within 10 days.

16. PRODUCER shall have exclusive control over the production, presentation and performance of the engagement hereunder, including, but not limited to, the details, means and methods employed in fulfilling each obligation of PRODUCER hereunder in all respects. PRODUCER shall have the sole right, as PRODUCER may see fit, to designate and change at any time the performing personnel other than the ARTIST(s) specifically named herein.

17. PURCHASER agrees (a) to comply promptly with PRODUCER's directions as to stage settings for the performance hereunder, (b) that no performers other than those to be furnished by PRODUCER hereunder will appear on or in connection with the engagement hereunder, (c) that no stage seats are to be sold or used without PRODUCER's prior written consent, and (d) that the entertainment presentation will not be included in a subscription or other type of series without the written consent of PRODUCER.

18. It is agreed that PRODUCER signs this contract as an independent contractor and not as an employee. This contract shall not, in any way be construed so as to create a partnership, or any kind of joint undertaking or venture between the parties hereto, nor make PRODUCER liable in whole or in part for any obligation that may be incurred by PURCHASER in PURCHASER's carrying out any of the provisions hereof or otherwise.

19. Nothing in this Agreement shall require the commission of any act contrary to law or to any rules or regulations of any union, guild or similar body having jurisdiction over the services and personnel to be furnished by PRODUCER to PURCHASER hereunder. If there is any conflict between any provision of this Agreement and any law, rule or regulation, such law, rule or regulation shall prevail and this Agreement shall be curtailed, modified, or limited only to the extent necessary to eliminate such conflict. PURCHASER agrees to comply with all regulations and requirements of any union(s) that may have jurisdiction over any of the said materials, facilities and personnel to be furnished by PURCHASER.

20. In the event of any inconsistency between the provisions of this contract and the provisions of any riders, addenda, exhibits or any other attachments hereto, the parties agree that the provisions most favorable to PRODUCER and ARTIST shall control.

21. PURCHASER hereby indemnifies and holds PRODUCER and ARTIST, as well as their respective agents, representatives, principals, employees, officers and directors, harmless from and against any loss, damage or expense, including reasonable attorney's fees, incurred or suffered by or threatened against PRODUCER or ARTIST or any of the foregoing in connection with or as a result of any claim for personel injury or property damage or otherwise brought by or on behalf of any third party person, firm or corporation as a result of or in connection with the engagement, which claim does not result from the active negligence of the ARTIST and/or PRODUCER.

22. William Morris Agency, Inc. acts herein only as agent for PRODUCER and is not responsible for any act of commission or omission on the part of either PRODUCER, ARTIST or PURCHASER. In furtherance thereof and for the benefit of William Morris Agency, it is agreed that neither PURCHASER nor PRODUCER will name or join William Morris Agency as a party in any civil action or suit arising out of, in connection with, or related to any act(s) of commission or omission of PURCHASER, ARTIST or PRODUCER.

23. This contract (a) cannot be assigned or transferred without the written consent of PRODUCER, (b) contains the sole and complete understanding of the parties hereto and (c) may not be amended, supplemented, varied or discharged, except by an instrument in writing signed by both parties. The validity, construction and effect of this contract shall be governed by the laws of the State of California, regardless of the place of performance. THE PERSON EXECUTING THIS AGREEMENT ON PURCHASER'S BEHALF WARRANTS HIS/HER AUTHORITY TO DO SO, AND SUCH PERSON HEREBY PERSONALLY   ASSUMES LIABILITY FOR THE PAYMENT OF SAID PRICE IN FULL. The terms "PRODUCER", "ARTIST" and "PURCHASER" as used herein shall include and apply to the singular, the plural and to all genders.

most major acts, they are actually a corporate entity controlled by the Smothers themselves. They contract to the William Morris Agency as the exclusive talent agency. I will have some contracts with Knave Productions relative to promotional materials and travel schedules but only after the contracts are signed. In this case I was representing The Maryland School for the Blind, so they are the "purchaser." Let's examine the five key points on this cover sheet.

1. This tells where the concert will be held. *Scaling* refers to a system where we pay a flat guaranteed fee and a percentage of the gate. We are paying a flat fee so there is no scaling.
2. The date of engagement, time of show and length of show.
3. Billing in this case refers to Headline Billing not payments.
4. The full price and key riders — internal ground transportation, two one-bedroom suites and three king single hotel rooms for two nights. It also points out that The Kingston Trio will be the opening act. I placed in the contract that the performers are to be available for some pre concert press and they will attend a meet and greet after the concert with my major donors.
5. The terms of payment are outlined.

Those are the basic points we discussed and agreed to on the phone and the remainder of the contract should deal with technical issues and support these points; however, like most contracts, they don't. Attached to this basic contract was a multiple page rider from Knave Productions which gave technical specifications for The Smothers Brothers stage set up and performer needs. The 12-page rider was obviously a standard form that was just attached to the cover contract; however, many items negotiated out of the original contract were left in the rider. I just took my pen and crossed out all items I did not agree with, putting my initials next to each one.

I made the changes in long hand and sent the contract back to the agency where it was accepted as corrected. If I had not made those corrections I would have been responsible for all the items I did not cross out. The argument that we had agreed I would not pay for airfare on the phone would not hold up in court when a written document was presented with my agreement to pay that fare. To quote the great Sam Goldwyn, "A verbal contract ain't worth the paper it's written on."

You have now seen an encapsulated version of the booking procedure for a major performer and you've had a chance to look at a really intimidating contract. We will revisit and refine much of this process in the next few chapters as we bring the entire process together. We will also adjust this procedure for smaller and larger concerts. What you do have at this point is a much more refined ability to develop an estimated budget for your planned event and that is where we are going in the next chapter.

Chapter 4
The First Budget

Since the performer and the venue are invariably the two most costly items in your budget, you are well on your way to estimating the cost of staging a major concert. Your budget is a collection of best estimates and it allows you to make reasonable projections as to the likelihood of success or failure. A realistic budget falls between an optimistic one and a pessimistic one. I generally draft all three types in order to get a sense of the possibilities. If you are considering acts at very different price levels it pays to draft separate budgets for comparison.

For all the mystery and apprehension about developing a budget, it is in fact a well organized estimate of the potential cost and the potential income. It is your roadmap for the event and it is not all that difficult to develop. The budget format I outline here should cover the basic plan for most concerts and you should be able to use this format as a template for your first event. Let's start with the expenses first:

1. The performer is the biggest single expense so let's begin there. I'm going to use the Ray Charles Concert for this sample budget so I'll plug in his on tour rate of $40,000.
2. The Meyerhoff Symphony Hall will cost $3,800 to rent. I plan to have a pre-concert VIP reception in the lobby (lobby rental $900) and an after-concert "meet and greet" for my major sponsors in the Green Room (Green Room rental $600). I would like to use

the Meyerhoff Box Office for all ticketing and I would additionally like to use Meyerhoff House Personnel for security, ticket
taking and ushering. (We will discuss why a little later but let's
just put them in the budget for now).
3. I've taken the outline of technical specifications supplied with
the riders and reviewed the lighting and sound requirements
with the shop steward at the Meyerhoff. He helped develop a list
of what is in place and what additionally needs to be rented. He
also supplied the names and addresses of several sound and
lighting contractors who often work with The Meyerhoff. I also
asked that he give me an estimate of the cost of union personnel
for this show. Almost all of the equipment was available through
the Meyerhoff and I called a lighting company to find out the cost
of two special follow spot lights.
4. In the contract from Ray Charles we agreed to supply a grand
piano ($450 from Meyerhoff) and a special Hammond Organ
($500 from a local music company). These costs, by the way,
include delivery, tuning and clearing after the concert.
5. If the budget will allow, I plan to hire a very experienced stage
and production manager to take care of all the technical specifications and to manage the stage during the show. This is not a
mandatory expense but it sure makes everything run like clock-
work. I'm building it into the budget with the hope it is affordable at $4,000.

That pretty much takes care of all the key production
expenses, so let's add them up and get a sense as to where our
budget stands.

Performer:
Ray Charles and his Band $40,000

Venue:
Meyerhoff Rental $3,800
Lobby Reception Rental 900
Green Room Rental 600
Box Office ticket printing 175
Box Office Service with charges 1,000
House Personnel
    (ushers, ticket takers, etc) 1,425
Security 300

House Sound 450
House Lights 450
Extra Lights 350
Piano Rental 450
Hammond Organ Rental 500
Estimated cost of union stage personnel . . .5,500
Stage Manager/Production specialist 4,000

Total $19,900

Total $59,900

We've taken care of the production costs but we still have other expenses to account for. Since Ray Charles only has a 70-minute stage show, we need to book an opening act. We know of several local acts that would be appropriate for a 30 to 40-minute opening. These acts would normally charge in the range of $1,500 to $3,500 for a show but we strongly believe that we can negotiate a price in the range of $1,000 since the local act would get to open for Ray Charles at a spectacular venue.

We plan to have a VIP reception for our major donors and for those people willing to pay extra for a special pre-show reception and preferred seating. We've set a goal of 250 people for our VIP reception the first year out. A few calls to caterers indicate that we can have quality heavy appetizers with wine and soft drinks for no more than $30 per person, tax and gratuity included. We also budget in an additional $400 for our after-show coffee and desserts at the meet and greet reception in the green room.

We want our own photographer for celebrity photos as well as follow up publicity photos for the local press ($500) and we will provide meals during the day for crew and volunteers to the tune of another ($500).

It is our intention to have the vast majority of our publicity and advertising donated but we still have a base line advertising budget of $1,500 for any advertising we must have but can't negotiate. It is also our experience that you can sometimes buy very little advertising and get a lot more donated; consequently, we need to have some cash if called for. We also have added $800 to our budget to cover the major banner for the stage listing all of our sponsors (approximately $600) and a ceremonial presentation check ($200).

We believe that a quality booklet program of the concert is a major selling tool for the concert next year as well as a thank you for this year's sponsors. We will talk more about the promotional aspects of the concert in Chapter 8 but we have committed to producing a quality printed program, flyers and a poster. We hope to have art and at least a portion of the printing donated but we have added $5,000 to our budget for printing.

We have grouped smaller incidentals such as flyer postage, picture frames for major donor photos, stationary, phone, sponsor letters, etc. into one category of incidentals rounded at $1,000. These additional expenses come to:

```
Opening Act . . . . . . . . . . . . . . . . . . . . . . . . .$1,000
Reception . . . (250 x $30) . . . . . . . . . . . . . . .7,500
Green Room Reception Catering . . . . . . . . . .400
Photographer . . . . . . . . . . . . . . . . . . . . . . . . 500
Crew Meals . . . . . . . . . . . . . . . . . . . . . . . . . .500
Advertising . . . . . . . . . . . . . . . . . . . . . . . . . .1,500
Banners, Ceremonial Check . . . . . . . . . . . . . .800
Printing . . . . . . . . . . . . . . . . . . . . . . . . . . . . .5,000
        Total . . . . . . . . . . . . . . . . . . . . . . . .$17,200
```

If we add this figure to our production figure of $59,900 we get a total of $77,100. I think that covers all of our expenses, but I've learned from experience to add a contingency for any costs we may have overlooked. If we need the money, it's in the budget. If we don't need the money, our profit is even better. I'm going to estimate 5% of our total cost as a contingency expense which will add another $3,865 to our projected expenses. Walking through our budget the first time we have a pretty good estimate that this concert would cost us $80,965 to stage. This estimate moved to the higher end of most projected costs, meaning we should be able to come in under this budget.

I know that's a lot of money but we need to look at the other side of the equation before we decide what we want to do. We need to project the potential income from this event.

We've done a careful search of sponsors in our area and we know that an event like this has several levels of sponsorship once the event is established. We are a new event and it will be very difficult for us to solicit the same donations as the already established events. We have decided that our sponsorship levels will be half the going rate. Our major sponsorship will be $25,000, Gold sponsorships will be $5,000 and Silver will be $2,500 each. You will see a detailed description as to how we value each sponsorship in the next chapter.

My committee estimated the sponsorships we could develop our first year out and came up with the following projection:

Major Sponsor	1 @ $25,000	$25,000
Gold Sponsor	4 @ $5,000	20,000
Silver Sponsor	4 @ $2,500	10,000
	Total	$55,000

We estimated our income from two sources — sponsors and ticket sales. As a rule of thumb it is my goal that the potential sale of tickets should basically cover the cost of the event. The sponsor dollars should all be profit.

When it comes to ticket pricing there are two basic strategies: charge the typical cost of tickets for a show of similar quality in your area or charge an inflated price since your event is a fund raiser. I believe in the first strategy for several reasons. When you need to sell a few thousand seats your prices must be competitive. People aren't stupid and most people that show up for your concert are not going to be there because of your cause. They will be there for the concert and they expect to pay a typical concert price.

On more than one occasion I've seen an organization host a major act that would sell several thousand seats at fair market which would be tickets running from $19 to $35 each. Instead they decide to charge something like $75 since it is supposed to be a fund raiser. Time after time I've seen the organization sell 100 to 300 tickets to their closest supporters and end up with an almost empty theatre and a major financial loss.

With the exception of a limited number of VIP tickets, which include a reception, all of my tickets follow the fair market value of tickets for similar concerts. Remember my goal is that income from ticket sales will cover the cost of putting on the concert; therefore, the income from sponsorships will be profit. This also gives me a natural limit on the kind of concert I can afford. What I mean by that is after my projected income for ticket sales is totaled it should be greater than the projected cost of production. In other words, if I project a total cost of $75,000 then my projected income from ticket sales should be $75,000 or more. If the projected income is less than the cost of the show, I am more than likely spending too much for the package.

Figuring out the correct price for tickets is not all that difficult. Examine a few weeks of newspaper ads in your area for concerts of similar quality. It's also wise to check the season rate sheets for local venues that have concert series. The Meyerhoff has five ticketing price levels, which we felt were too much trouble to advertise, so we reduced the number to three levels with the exception of the VIP tickets.

Most venues have a chart that reflects typical pricing scales for seating. The chart below shows the price and seating layout for the Meyerhoff Symphony Hall. We have simplified this pricing structure so that the least expensive seats are the Terrace (second balcony) seating, which is the highest point of the theatre. There are 530 of these seats and they will sell for $18.50 each. Rows AA through HH are in the back of the orchestra and they are covered by the 1st Balcony directly above and they will be our mid-price tickets at $27.50. There are 320 of these seats available for sale. The largest number of seats are in the Orchestra A through Z for 995, the Grand Tier for 376 seats and the boxes for an additional 192. That gives us a total of 1,589 seats that will sell for $35 each. I estimate that 150 of these seats will be part of the donor package for sponsors at the VIP level but they will still have an income value of $35 each. One hundred additional seats will be sold as VIP seats for $125 so our total looks like the following:

530 seats @ $18.50	=	$9,805
320 seats @ $27.50	=	$8,800
1,489 seats @ $35.00	=	$52,115
100 seats @ $125.00	=	$12,500
2,439 seats total	=	$83,220

Since our projected costs come to $80,965 it appears that our projected income from ticket sales gives us a slight profit. We've passed the first rough budget test. According to our figures, the concert will basically pay for itself with ticket sales and our sponsor income should be all profit. Now this is a first draft budget and you can be certain that the numbers will change; however, we are trying to lay down good approximations in order to predict the potential success or failure of this first venture. If the numbers didn't work at this stage there would be little point in moving forward. You would stop and re-examine your options. Perhaps your hall is too small for your act and you need to move up to a larger venue. Perhaps your act is too expensive and you need to set your sights and budget lower. The budget process is a way for you to balance possibilities. Within the last month I went to a great concert in a venue that had about 1,000 seats. It was a sellout but the organization lost money because the act was too expensive for the hall. Running through a budget process like this would have told them as much. Instead they needed about $30,000 of sponsor money to cover expenses. They only had a sellout crowd, a lovely event and $25,000 in sponsor money. They lost $5,000. Not the end of the world but not necessary if they had spent a bit more time in budget planning. Imagine what would have happened if they hadn't had a sellout!

At this stage our first budget suggests that we are basically on target for a successful event. We have a framework in which we can operate but we have a lot of planning to do yet. These are pretty good approximations but approximations nonetheless, we are not quite ready to sign contracts but we are getting there. We know that we can, at best, break even with ticket sales but we want to do more than break even. This concert is supposed to be a fund raiser not a "break-even event." We need to make money and we need sponsors in order to do that.

Chapter 5
The Sponsors

What's the difference between professional promoters and fund raisers when it comes to concerts? Most promoters make or lose their profit by selling seats; whereas, most fund raisers make or lose their profit by involving sponsors. One of the great benefits of concerts as fund raisers for an organization is that they create opportunities to involve new sponsors for your organization. There are so many good causes soliciting support from corporate America that it is often difficult to make your organization stand out from the others. Corporations often receive several requests each *day* from local non-profits in search of corporate dollars.

As fund raisers, we know that our cause or organization is worthwhile and we know that cause merits support; however, the same is true for most of our peers. Part of our goal is to separate ourselves out, at least enough for a potential supporter to examine our support statement. I've spent many years on the other side of the aisle, receiving requests for support from non-profits and I understand what corporate donors are dealing with when it comes to these multiple requests. People are people, and they don't want to be in the position of having to say "No," time after time to organizations that they more than likely value. What happens over time is that the potential corporate donor really doesn't hear the details of your request. As a given, they will more than likely assume your cause is worthy; however, they are already supporting a certain number of other worthwhile causes and that's the extent of their support. In other words, it isn't enough that you are worthy of support. You are not going to get their attention by a reasoned approach. It may not be a story we want to accept but it's a fact. There is a point at which many donors switch off their hearing for survival. It's not especially a bad thing, it just is.

Concerts have a special cache when it comes to bringing on otherwise disinterested sponsors. Why? Because you start to deal with things that interest the potential sponsor at an entirely different level. Time after time, I've been able to get through previously closed doors not because the sponsor is interested in me or my cause but because I'm offering the chance for that sponsor to meet and greet someone who pushes all of their buttons. If I'm bringing Ray Charles to town and the sponsor *loves* Ray Charles — or The Oak Ridge Boys or whomever my featured act is — then I'm bringing them a story they want to hear. They will have the chance to put their name on a program with Ray and be part of the in-crowd and even get a photo with Ray for their office wall. Remember, people are people, and we all have our interests, our hobbies and our passions. Celebrity is a valuable commodity and we need to recognize that fact if we are to market it correctly. Far too often I've seen golden opportunities sold as tin foil trinkets.

You can have many different levels of sponsorship as your event grows but I try to keep it very simple to start. Until you are well established I recommend you have one major sponsor, and as many gold sponsors and silver sponsors as you can bring on board. VIP ticket buyers are not sponsors but they are an important part of your sponsorship mix and they are highly profitable. You need to find out what sponsorships cost in your area and price yours accordingly. When we first staged a concert for The Maryland School for the Blind, I contacted a few major organizations in our area that sponsored concerts and asked what they charged for their sponsorships. As a start-up event, I estimated that we should be charging about half of the rate for an already established and successful event. I wanted to get people in the door as sponsors with the hope they would be happy and grow with us over the years.

The base of the sponsorship pyramid is the VIP reception. This is really a fund raiser within a fund raiser. It is held about an hour and a half before the concert starts and it is held either at your venue or someplace very close by. It must be within a short walk of your event. The reception itself must be elegant and it must be visible. The whole point is to have an event that is a step up from the main event. That's marketing! Keeping up with the Joneses is that as they move up socially their neighbors wish to do the same. Sensible? Maybe not, but it seems to be the way things work.

If a lobby or major meeting room is not available, receptions can be in a nearby museum, an historic building, the lobby of an elegant but closed business building in the area, even tents erected close to your venue. When Cystic Fibrosis held the first concert at Pier Six in Baltimore, they got the governor to loan the state yacht for the reception. The yacht was moored at a pier several hundred feet from the venue and created a spectacular site for that VIP reception.

The reception is not a place to cut corners. This is not the place to use "pigs in a blanket" because they are cheap. This is the place you are going to reward your sponsors and recruit new sponsors for future events. As a general rule, I hire a first-rate caterer and I try to provide something new and exciting. This is not another wedding reception with rumaki or canned stuffed mushrooms. Lovely displays of unusual and beautiful finger food should be the rule. Champagne and wine are always my first choice, with some beer, soda and sparkling water in support. I've never felt the need for mixed drinks.

Do not run out of food or wine. You are making a fortune on every VIP ticket sold and it is plain stupid to cheat people who've paid extra to be treated well. Remember, you are trying to make a profit *and* make friends. You want people to say "Wow! That was a great event," when they leave. Most importantly, those attending your VIP reception have self selected as potentially high-level donors. They are already paying $125 a seat for a $35 ticket and some wine. Make them happy not angry. My wife and I recently went to see Kenny G at a benefit concert. The concert was great but the pre-concert reception at $150 a ticket was overcrowded, and had long lines at too few food stations with mid-level food. I was aghast when they ran out of wine about half way through the reception. We certainly will go see Kenny G again but I will never attend an event hosted by that organization, nor am I inclined to be involved with them. Their cause is worthy but so are many similar organizations and I would rather be involved with an organization that values my patronage.

VIP ticket holders also get preferred seating. They get the best seats in the house and why not? They're paying for them.

You've rented the entire Symphony Hall, all 3,000 seats let's say; consequently, all the seats cost the same. You decide which seats and how many sell for $18.50 or $27.50 or $35 but the seats all cost the same: the true cost per seat equals the cost of the Hall divided by the number of seats. If the venue will cost $15,000 to rent and you have 3,000 seats then the cost per seat is $5. Needless to say, you make a lot of money when you sell one of those seats for $125.

In addition to the catering and the preferred seating, VIPs get to mix with the celebrities you invite to your reception. The main act rarely appears at this reception since they like to make their first entrance of the night on stage; however, there are always exceptions. The Hard Travelers always open the show for their annual Cystic Fibrosis benefit but they make a point of mixing at the pre concert VIP reception. They want to thank all the fans who've chosen to pay extra to support their favorite charity. They are shaking hands, smiling in group photos and making hundreds of new friends every year. As we will discuss later, I also make sure we have some local political, sports and media celebrities on hand for mixing and adding a touch of importance.

If the VIP reception is the base of the pyramid, then the after concert meet and greet with the featured performer is the pinnacle. This is a short reception, usually 20 to 30 minutes, held shortly after the concert. It is often the case that wine and light canapés may be served although I prefer to serve coffee and interesting desserts. These receptions are held late at night and it is not a good time to be serving drinks.

The performer usually has time to change before coming to mix and chat with your selected guests. I always have a photographer on hand for small group photos of sponsors with the star. These photos are hand delivered to our major sponsors a week or two after the concert. This event is the top reward for your top sponsors. It is meant to be exclusive or else it isn't special. You must be firm in limiting the number of people attending. In particular you may not have board members or lower-level sponsors elbowing their way into this private reception. You must be firm and you must have the meet and greet in your contract if you expect the artist to appear. Most artists will limit the number of people allowed to attend and they will limit the amount of time they will spend. A general rule of thumb is something like no more than 50 people and 20 minutes of time. The event must be held in a place that is secure in order to control which people may enter and it should be held in an intimate setting so that everyone feels special. We will talk more about the meet and greet later as it is a very powerful tool for moving sponsors from one level of sponsorship to a higher level.

Now that we understand VIP tickets and the meet and greet let's look at a typical breakdown of sponsorships. This chart comes from a Smothers Brothers and Kingston Trio Concert held in 1998.

VIP Ticket
$125
Pre-concert reception and preferential reserved seating

Silver Sponsor
$2,500
Four VIP tickets to our pre-concert reception
with preferential reserved seating
Half page ad in our concert program
Some promotional materials from concert

Gold Sponsor
$5,000
Eight VIP tickets to our pre-concert reception
with preferential reserved seating
Full page ad in our concert program
Company logo in most pre-concert media advertising
Personalized promotional materials from concert
Private after-concert reception with performers for two people

Major Sponsor
$25,000
Twenty-four VIP tickets to our pre-concert reception
with preferential reserved seating
Featured as presenter in all media and program advertising
Banner at concert as presenter
Full page ad in program
Stage appearance to present check
for total dollars raised for concert
Personalized promotional materials from concert
Private after-concert reception with performers for eight people

The personalized promotional materials I mention are usually autographed programs and posters from the concert. I have these ready to be autographed before the show begins, usually in the performer's dressing room. For the major sponsor I get the performer to autograph a poster and then I usually add the signatures of all the major players involved with a big "Thank You" and the firm's name in the middle. I then have the poster framed professionally. There is nothing like walking into the offices of a major sponsor and seeing your poster, or even better posters, hanging in a prominent place for all to see. They get to show their civic responsibility and you get the name of your organization linked with a very successful firm. Everybody wins.

Once you've established your basic levels of sponsorship it's time to start shopping for sponsors. First and foremost you should approach your board of directors. I usually make a presentation and then I give out a single-page form which outlines the levels of sponsorship. I make it clear that VIP tickets are not sponsorships but I encourage board members to help sell these tickets to friends and associates. I ask board members to bring their companies on as sponsors and I ask them to recommend other potential corporate sponsors. I make it clear that I will gladly make the presentation if they will arrange the meeting.

The next obvious source of sponsorships are companies that do business with your organization. Suppliers, bankers, accounting firms, the company managing your employee retirement funds, insurance agents, printers, consultants and any other organization that wants your business. The approach to these companies varies, although personal contacts are always the best. If you have a board member who is a very good customer of one of these firms, try to get them to make the request. When you have a relationship with a company, even a tenuous one, figure out the best way to develop that relationship. A fairly simple approach that I use for many of my events is a letter to outline what our sponsorship levels are; however, that letter is followed up with a phone call in order to develop the sponsorship. I've attached two sample letters at the end of this chapter.

The most difficult sponsor to develop is the "cold call," an organization with which you can find no personal relationship. Most major cities have a business journal of some sort and most produce an annual listing of major business groupings in that area along with the names and addresses of major officers. In our area it is the *Baltimore Business Journal* and they produce an annual listing of business leaders by type. The listings include the largest privately held companies, accounting firms, law firms, etc. This issue is one of my major "cold call" prospecting tools. I review the lists with board members or senior members or our production team. If I can figure out a contact or way to develop a personal introduction to any of these organizations I try to develop that contact. If there is no contact I use a personalized letter and follow up four to seven days later with a phone call. Although this is a very low return source of sponsors, it is a source and each of these sponsors is a corporate sponsor. It is a foot in the door with a new sponsor and I have the chance to grow that sponsorship over the next few years. Three hundred letters with a 1% return is three new sponsors to grow for that year. Most importantly, remember that the concert is a tool to bring the sponsor on board, a chance for them to size you up, to decide if you are the kind of organization they want to be involved with. With proper management, sponsors will interact with your organization all year long. They can be a source of corporate dollars, new individual donors who get to know you through the corporation, volunteers, new board members and contacts to other corporations. My best source of corporate sponsors is other corporate sponsors. The investment in time is well worth the potential outcome. I've also attached a "cold call" letter at the end of this chapter for your reference. You will notice that I've rolled several selling points together in one package and you will notice that my approach is not "Please help us because we need the charity." I try to maintain a sense of "This is a great opportunity for you to become involved with a great event and a great organization."

February 6, 1998

Board Member
Address
Address

Dear last name,

Since taking over as Director of Development I've made a point of not involving board members in late night phone parties or many of the annoying details of fund raising. I respect your time and your position; therefore, I've been holding you in reserve so that we can make the best use of your resources. Now the time has come.

I need each and every board member to get a sponsor for our Concert. Some of you are already Concert sponsors and some of you are sponsors of our Golf Tournament. In fact, a few of you sponsor both and we are very grateful; however, I need everyone to step up to the plate if we are to move to the next level. I need you to get your organization to become a sponsor or approach one of your friends or business contacts.

I've waited until we had an event that you could present with pride, knowing full well that your friends and associates will be delighted with the quality program we will present. We had a winner our first year out of the blocks and this concert will be even better. I've spoken with the Governor's office and both Governor and Mrs. Glendening plan to attend. We will have more celebrity guests, more media coverage and I expect a sell out crowd.

To those of you already sponsoring, thank you again for your support. I will be glad to help the rest of you in any way I can. I'll even make "the ask" if you want, but you need to get me in the door. We need to work together until we identify a sponsor from each board member. I believe each and every one of our sponsors will be glad they joined us, but I need your help to get them to the concert. Each of you will hear from me within the next few weeks, so please start thinking about your sponsor now.

Thanks,

Jim Hollan

Director of Development

PS - I will contact each of you about our pending legislation as soon as we have a bill number. That should be within the next few days.

January 23, 1997

Mary Harrington
First National Bank
P.O.Box 1596
Baltimore, NM 21203

Dear Mary,

As a follow up to our brief conversation after the Board of Directors meeting I'm writing to ask that First National Bank consider being a Gold or Silver sponsor for the upcoming Ray Charles Concert. It's especially difficult to get the "first" event off the ground, consequently, it's a time we look to our closest supporters for leadership.

As you know the Governor and Mrs. Glendening have agreed to co-chair this event and we expect to have a number of celebrities at our pre concert champagne reception at The Meyerhoff. I am talking to both Marty Bass and WJZ 13 to act as our media sponsor as well as *The Baltimore Sun* and *The Daily Record*.

This is going to be a first class event, the kind of event your organization will be proud to sponsor; moreover, it's going to be a lot of fun. I know you are always there for us, Mary, and I appreciate any efforts you can make on our behalf as we try to launch this first annual event. Let me know if I can answer any questions or provide any additional information. Thanks.

Yours

Jim Hollan

January 30, 1997

Mr. Robert XXXXXX
XXXXXXXXXXXXX
XXXXXXXXXXXXX
XXXXXXXXXXXXX

Dear Mr. XXXXXX

On Friday evening, June 20, 1997 the one and only Ray Charles will present a concert at The Meyerhoff Symphony Hall to benefit The Maryland School for the Blind. Governor and Mrs. Parris Glendening, our honorary chairs, will be joined by a number of other celebrities in this first annual event to recognize the contributions of this outstanding school. We need your help.

The Maryland School for the Blind is not a state agency. Founded in 1853, we are a private, nonprofit organization serving blind and visually impaired children in every county of the state, every day of the week. I'm proud to say that we have a world wide reputation for excellence and innovation.

I'm writing to ask that you become involved as a Silver or Gold sponsor for this extraordinary event. You will be featured in all pre concert advertising as well as the concert program; you will receive preferential reserved seating and be invited to our private champagne reception with other major sponsors and celebrity guests at, The Meyerhoff prior to the concert.

I need your help if we are to continue providing the many services that blind and visually impaired children need and deserve. Will you help us? Will you step forward in our time of need. Will you join with other leaders in the public and private sector from all across Maryland as we launch this First Annual Concert to benefit The Maryland School for the Blind?

Yours,

Jim Hollan
Director of Development

Chapter 6
Media Sponsors

The cost of advertising and promoting a major concert can easily exceed the cost of hiring the artist and venue combined. The saving grace, fortunately, comes in the form of media sponsors. In a nutshell a media sponsor contributes advertising instead of dollars. Since major advertising is fundamental to the success of most every concert, media sponsors are a key ingredient to the mix of sponsors needed for success.

When you negotiate with a regular sponsor, the benefits are built around dollars contributed. With a media sponsor, the benefits are built around the amount of space donated and the kind of coverage contributed; consequently, the fine line between different levels of sponsorship becomes less clear. If a regular sponsor donates $5,000 in cash you get $5,000 in your hand to do with what you will. When a media sponsor donates $5,000 worth of advertising, it's not very clear what you have. Every media outlet has a price list of cost for advertising and no media outlet lives by the fixed prices on that list. It is the rule for advertising to be sold or discounted so that a media salesperson can say, "Here is our price list and you can see that a page ad will cost you $500 to run. If you get three of these ads, I'll give you a fourth free and if you buy seven ads I'll give you three additional for free." Don't worry about the math in this example, just focus on the process. Salespeople need something to work with and the price list needs to be structured in such a way that prices go down as frequency increases. There is a substantial difference in giving $5,000 cash and $5,000 worth of advertising space. The actual cost of the space, based on when the ads are run may amount to several dollars, not several thousand dollars. The point is that you will be negotiating for more than the posted retail value of ads when you negotiate with your potential media sponsors. It's not mandatory that you know these rates, but, like chicken soup, it couldn't hurt.

Once again, my goal is to make this a win-win situation for everyone. I want the media sponsors to be glad that they signed on to sponsor our event. I want them to get positive recognition for their sponsorship. I want them to feel good about my event and I want them to become more and more involved over time so that *my* event eventually becomes *their* event. The best way to do this is to make sure that they are appropriately acknowledged before, during and after the concert itself. Let them know how much you value their support and acknowledge how important that support is to the success of your event.

Before you request support, take the time to at least know something about your potential media sponsor. Find the right person to ask at the sponsoring organization and be prepared to ask for some specifics rather than a general "We want you to be our sponsor." Find out if any of your board members are involved with the media sponsor already and ask them to help make the request. I've spoken with many media representatives over the years and all agree that the very best way to get sponsorship from their organization is to get a major customer of theirs to do the asking. It's common sense if you think about it. If you were a station manager and received a request for free media sponsorship from a well meaning group you respect but don't really have any relationship with and you also receive a request for support from one of your major advertisers who sits on the board of directors of an equally important non profit, whom are you most likely to sponsor? Once again the easier you make it for your potential sponsor to say "yes" the more likely they are to actually say "yes."

Television — When I can, I look for a major TV station to act as a major media sponsor. I ask the station to make my event a special promotion for them. I ask for on-air support prior to the concert. I ask them to develop the ads for our program and I usually request that one of their news personalities act as our master of ceremonies for the evening. This is a point where scheduling can be a problem so you want to get to the station as soon as possible.

All geographic areas have a media guide that will tell you who does what at each station. If you can't locate one, just call the station and ask them to send you a copy as this brochure usually gives you some pointers on approaching the station for different kinds of sponsorship. A phone call to the correct person will give you a rough sense as to whether or not your request is reasonable and it will usually end in a request for a letter outlining the details of your event. Make sure you ask how long it will take for a decision once the letter is received, then follow up a week or so after that deadline. At many stations the decision to sponsor an event is made first by station management, then the level of station involvement is discussed. The selection of a station celebrity is the last step in the process.

The television station will generally produce an ad as part of their sponsorship and they will run the ad at various times, especially very early in the morning and very late at night. You want to convince them to run your ad as often as possible and you want them to run the ad during some of their best time spots. Your goal is to get your ad on television as early as possible, perhaps eight or 10 weeks before your event and you want the frequency to increase as you get closer to your event.

In addition to the ad you want "on-air support" for your event. That includes things like news celebrities discussing your concert in the weeks before the event or an interview with someone in your organization about the organization itself with a plug for the upcoming concert. You can often (but not always) get your act to agree to interviews if they are in town a day or two before your show and a good interview can have a remarkable result. The Smothers Brothers came into Baltimore the night before our show and agreed to an on-air interview with our network media sponsor. The interview was very funny and very clever and the phones were ringing off the hook the next morning for hundreds of additional ticket sales. It was also an eye opener to see the response from the staff at the television station. Everybody recognized The Smothers and came to say "Hello," or get a photo, including all the folks I watched on TV every evening. Local celebrities are also fans and they were just as excited to see other celebrities as we were. Another reminder that people are just people.

Make sure you ask for coverage the day of and day after the event. Although the former sells very few tickets and the latter clearly sells none, you still want to create a sense of excitement about your event that will carry through to the following year. Remember that your goal is more than ticket sales or income. You want people to recognize that your organization is a major player in your area. What better way than having the morning news tell everyone how great your event was?

By the way, you will have *one* television sponsor. Stations are competitive and with very rare exceptions they do not sponsor an event that is already being sponsored by another station.

Radio — All major television networks program for all demographic groups; consequently, any major network will likely suit your purposes as a sponsor. The demographics for radio stations, on the other hand, are often very specific. Some radio stations are all talk, some oldies, some country, some classical, some just play Top 40. Some cater to the young, others cater to the old. It's pretty difficult to select the wrong kind of network television sponsor but fairly easy to select the wrong kind of radio station. Even more important is the fact that most radio stations don't have the demographic and advertising impact of television. Notice I said *most*, not all.

You need to select a station that will reach the kind of audience you hope to attract to your concert. It's silly to have a rock and roll oldies station sponsor a country music concert and vice versa. In the Baltimore area The Hard Travelers and Friends hooked up with WPOC, a local country music station, when both the concert and the station were in the formative stages. WPOC has made this annual event the major annual promotion for their station. They not only advertise the concert for months ahead of time but they involve other station sponsors and fans in concert events. It is a marriage made in heaven, so much so that I believe this is the rare exception where the radio sponsorship has more impact than the television sponsorship.

With an act like Ray Charles I had a major TV sponsor but no obvious radio sponsor. I did have a number of smaller stations that wanted to be involved. I donated tickets to these stations to be used as prizes and the stations ran contests and a lot of free air time about the concert. Another win-win situation. Once again, you need to check the local advertising index in order to get accurate numbers on the listening audience of your area radio stations. Some stations are so small that they will actually solicit you to be a sponsor and you might find yourself having to say "No." A station with a listening audience of several hundred is not going to help you very much. Crazy world isn't it?

Press — Ads in papers create excitement. They set the tone for your event and slowly build to a crescendo just before the concert. When you negotiate a major press sponsor you must get a series of ads that start early and build in frequency. The problem is that most papers are thinking in terms of a few ads and you are thinking of many.

You must understand that papers are approached all the time for free advertising for a good cause. At the same time, they make their money from advertising. It's a classic dilemma. When they agree to sponsor an event they tend to think in terms of a few ads. It is your job to get them thinking in terms of many ads. To that end the best advice I can give you is to help the paper think in terms of not just contributing ad space, you must help them think of this as a positive event they want to be involved with. Rather than some free ads for *your* event, get them thinking about promoting *their* event. With all of your media sponsors, tell them that you want a sellout if their name is associated with this event and a few more free ads from each might make that sellout happen.

You can, and likely will, have more than one media sponsor from papers and magazines. The level of support may be different and your acknowledgement of that support needs to reflect that difference. If a major metro newspaper supports your concert with several dozen ads over the course of many weeks, you need to acknowledge that level of support at a different level than the local weekly that gives you two announcements.

Radio and television stations will generally produce an ad to use for your event, but most papers and magazines will ask you to have an ad prepared for them. We will discuss ways to get these ads donated by graphic or advertising companies in the next chapter; however, remember that the biggest element in your ad is not your organization name but the name of the performer. Your main goal for the concert is not delivering a message about your organization. Your main goal is to get people to come to your concert and they will come to see the performer; consequently, that is the lead in all your ads.

Now that I've told you what you want from media sponsors let me tell you that you will get turned down cold by many of them, especially in your first year when you are nothing more than a packet of promises. Use who and what you know to get inside an organization. As mentioned above, use your board members who are advertisers when you can; however, you are going to get turned down and you might as well be prepared for it. It's generally not personal, just the reality of too many good organizations looking for free support from media companies that can only give so much. Do the best you can and keep growing. Almost all the big success stories started out with the bare minimum in media support. Remember that we are growing an event and that means everything from media support to the profits generated. It takes years to get from level to level and you are not going to start at the top. The end result is absolutely worth the effort, but don't overlook the dollar value of even start-up events. I make a point of calculating the dollar value of advertising for all of the ads donated for our events so that we have an accurate sense of total contributions. As an example, we were turned down by *The Baltimore Sun* as a media sponsor for a new concert series we planned. We were successful, however, in recruiting the publisher of 13 different small "local" papers in the area, most of them weeklies. The publisher agreed to run four quarter-page ads in each of his papers over a two-month period. The ads would be staggered over time and the fact is that he actually ended up running more than the promised number of ads, as the company became more committed to the event as we approached the concert date. My board members were disappointed that *The Sun* had not signed on as a sponsor. Many took it much too personally and some interpreted it as a sign that our event was not worth promoting in a major newspaper. Sadly, many of them undervalued the contributions of our smaller publisher who was running ads in all his smaller papers. That tuned changed when I presented the value of those ads in our after-concert summary. This publisher ended up donating over $27,000 worth of advertising in addition to a number of feature stories and an excellent follow-up piece on the concert and our organization. The advertising sold tickets to our concert; the features helped develop the positive public image of our organization.

With this general sense of media coverage you should sit down and outline a basic strategy for approaching potential media sponsors in your area. Develop an "A" list, a "B" list and a "C" list. Develop a first choice in each key media area. Choose a potential host or hostess for the evening, if appropriate, and work on that source. Remember that you can't have the evening news anchor from ABC in your area as host if you expect NBC to be your major media sponsor. Figure out whom is best suited to make the ask for this sponsorship and collect your presentation material.

After you locate your major sponsors, move down the list to your secondary sponsors. In our area we have a number of business weeklies, specialized newspapers, very small local newspapers and several regional magazines. We work through all of them for some coverage of our events and we have various levels of success. It is your job to develop a list of priorities and a plan of attack. When you get a commitment from a large sponsor, use that commitment to help bring on smaller sponsors or sponsors of similar stature. I've attached a few examples of letters requesting support but you must keep adjusting the letters as you bring other sponsors or celebrities on board. Many smaller sponsors will come on board because they want to be like the bigger sponsors. The point here is that you start your sponsorship requests from the top and work down. You must also start well in advance of your event, a year is not unreasonable so that you have time to move across a field of several major media sponsors if you are turned down by some.

Don't take media sponsorships for granted. It doesn't matter how good or how special your concert is. If nobody knows you are having a concert you will fail. If you have to pay for all of your advertising then your bottom line profits will be eaten up. Media sponsors are a key to your financial and public image success.

The best way to approach potential sponsors is person to person. The best person to approach a potential sponsor is an active customer of that sponsor. When you don't have a contact, a letter will work as a first step and I've attached a few generic letters that you might find useful. I don't pretend that they are great literature, but they do illustrate my attempts at personalizing and humanizing a letter to someone I barely know.

Fax

From: Jim Hollan
             The Maryland School for the Blind
             3501 Taylor Avenue
             Baltimore, Maryland 21236-4499
             410/444-5000 ext.288
             410/426-2590

To: Lori XXXXX
             XXXXXXXXXX

Dear Lori,

The Maryland School for the Blind is about to launch our first major concert featuring Ray Charles at The Meyerhoff Symphony on Friday, June 20, 1997. Governor and Mrs. Glendening have agreed to be our honorary co-chairs and Smith, Sommerville and Case, with headquarters here in Baltimore, have stepped forward as our major banner sponsor. We are actively signing on support at present but Gold and Silver sponsors already include BG&E, CSX, Edgemark Systems and Payne Weber. Even our opening act, Deanna Bogart, is a home grown performer who has just released her third album and is ready to "break out" on the national scene according to sources like *Cashbox* and *Downbeat*.

All I need to make this a knock out event is for WMAR-TV to sign on as our major media sponsor. At this point, Lori, I would like to ask for everything including the kitchen sink but the fact is I want a good selection of on screen support. We need a promo spot or two produced by you guys and some chit-chat going on air about the upcoming concert, perhaps tie ins like Deanna Bogart on Rodericks for Breakfast, etc. I want one of your key folks to be our MC the night of the concert and I want this to be the kind of event you love promoting - I want you to make it yours.

I'm negotiating with Patuxent Publishing and waiting to here back from *The Daily Record*. Tippy Martinez has already said he plans to attend our VIP Pre Concert Champagne Reception and I'm in the process of contacting other celebrities at this very moment. I expect to have some other notables in attendance.

Needless to say, WMAR-TV would be in all advertising, flyers and promotions. They would also have a page in our 36 page program and anything else I can think of to make you glad you came on board. I'll also make sure I include some tickets for our VIP reception. Let's do this Lori. It should actually be a lot of fun....

Jim Hollan

Fax

From: Jim Hollan
         The Maryland School for the Blind
         3501 Taylor Avenue
         Baltimore, Maryland 21236-4499
         410/444-5000 ext.288
         410/426-2590

To: Darlene XXXXX
         XXXXXXXXXX
         XXXXXXXXXX

Hi Darlene,

I'd like to get you guys to act as the media sponsor for our first major concert fund raising event. We have Ray Charles in concert on June 20, 1997 at The Meyerhoff. The Governor and Mrs. Glendening have agreed to act as Honorary Chairs and Smith, Sommervile & Case have signed on as our major sponsors.

I've just started soliciting my sponsors but (based on personal contacts and Board representation) I expect to have a number of major Baltimore and Maryland sponsors. We are a private, non profit, serving Maryland for 144 years and this is our first major event. I've asked WJZ-TV to act as sponsor and provide the master of ceremonies.

Operating on the thinnest of budgets, your agreement to provide ad space for free and give us what plugs can be gotten would help insure a successful first event. I would list *The Baltimore Sun* as our sponsor in all ads, brochures, flyers, posters and the program. I would additionally provide a full page ad in the Concert Program and provide some tickets for our Pre Concert Champagne Reception at The Meyerhoff.

So you'll help us out here?

Jim

Chapter 7
Art & Advertising

If you look marvelous you are marvelous, or put another way, if you are staging a first class event you must act and look first class. Good design is not something you can knock off in your spare time. It requires not only talent, but planning and coordination. Most importantly, the design of your event should be linked not only for consistency but also for cost savings.

I try to get the art work donated whenever I can and I must admit that it is generally not all that difficult to do. I've approached graphics or advertising agencies a number of times and asked them to develop a package for my event. I ask them to donate the project and I suggest that they use this project as one of their competition pieces. Many firms enter trade competitions in the graphics and advertising fields and they use the successful results of these competitions in their own advertising and marketing. I offer them a recognized name in terms of the performer and the chance to develop the kind of program they consider good enough to enter in competition against their professional peers. It's a strategy that has worked on more than one occasion.

If your organization is big enough to support the regular use of a graphics firm, this is a good chance to ask them for a donation of their talents. It's amazing how much easier it is to get a donation of services rather than a donation of money. If firms are off the beaten track, then try the art department at a local college or university. With enough lead time you might get one of the classes to adopt your project as a class project. Artists are everywhere and underutilized; they are often delighted to have the opportunity to reach a new audience. It's your job to make sure that the art they donated is presented well.

I am far too lazy to reinvent the wheel and not nearly talented enough to develop great design concepts. What I can do is keep clip files for ads, programs, flyers and clever design. Whenever I see something I like I just clip it out and stick it in one of my files. I especially like very generic ads as they offer the greatest opportunity for adaptation. When it's time for my event, I thumb through these folders and try to develop some rough ways these ads may relate to my upcoming concert. When talking with a potential designer it is extraordinarily helpful to point to examples rather than try to explain abstract concepts that are floating around in your head. Get in the habit of clipping now, you'll be real glad down the road.

You may or may not have a theme for your art. Sometimes it works and sometimes it doesn't. It may be that the feature performer alone is the focus of your art. It may be that a clever element in your program ties it all together. The Hard Travelers concerts to benefit Cystic Fibrosis have been very successful in tying hit tunes from their featured artists together with an appropriate element of their mission. They used the hit song "Angels Among Us" as a theme when they featured the group Alabama and I still remember the electric moment when The Oak Ridge Boys sang the theme song several years ago for the "Thank God for Kids" concert. You'll see examples of both theme and artist in the following pages.

The key element for your art package is the base art you will use in your newsprint ads. You want an ad that will stand on its own, can be adapted for several sizes and one that allows sponsor logos to be dropped in without ruining the overall effect. The more you can use one ad, the better off you are going to be. You will need different sizes to fit the different needs of media sponsors who run various formats for ads. If your experience is anything like mine, you will likely add sponsors once your campaign is under way and you will need the flexibility to just drop in a new logo or two as promised in your sponsor package. It is highly unlikely that anyone is going to design a large range of ads for you so flexibility in the initial design is a key.

After the basic ad is designed you want to develop a flyer and/or poster. Sometimes this will be the same art with some modest adjustment. At other times it may be completely different art. You must advertise, advertise, advertise before your event if you want to insure success. I use flyers for my in-house mail list as reminders and I try to develop flyers that can double as small posters. If your budget allows, I encourage full size posters. Although expensive, they create a real sense of professionalism about your event. It is also my custom to get the performers to sign a number of these posters which I then use as special thank you gifts for my major sponsors. Planning for the future, you should get some extra posters signed and put them away for years down the road when you can auction off posters from each of the previous concerts. They become collectibles in their own right, generating additional bonus dollars and interest, so putting a few aside is an investment in your future.

In lieu of a flyer, I've taken some poster design and turned the poster into a full color postcard with the concert information on the address side. I still see some of these lovely postcards hanging on refrigerators and bulletin boards.

I've attached some typical ads and variations from The Ray Charles Concert and The Smothers Brothers Concert. Notice how the base ad for each gets a slightly different spin based on where and when it is used. Some ads are adjusted just for size, some have sponsor names dropped in and some are used as flyers. The art for The Smothers Brothers concert was donated by a friend and was so bright and colorful that we made it into a post card with detailed concert info and telephone numbers on the back. I'm presenting these ads not particularly as great art but as a typical and straightforward way to get your story out to the media. The photos we used came from the performers' promotion packets. We made a point of sending these photos out with our key mailings to the press and you can see the impact an announcement has in the paper when a photo is featured with the story. It is often the case that you must pay for additional promotional photos from the artist. It is a good investment and we generally get 50 or 100 copies of each of two or three different photos.

If you look closely at the attached sampling of ads you will notice that we are also included in the calendar section of a magazine. Most papers and magazines run these sections but you must get your material out several months ahead of time. We roll out at least three different press releases along with a photo for all print announcements starting four to five months before the concert. The second round goes out three months before and the third round about two months before. We intersperse these regular press releases with at least two reminder announcements. I've attached a typical press release and a sample reminder. Great coverage does not happen by accident. It takes careful planning and timing. Identify your markets early on, set a plan for mailings with a calendar, then follow the plan so that each source receives four or five notices from you prior to your event. We probably mail in the range of 200 or 300 photos out prior to an event at a cost of perhaps $200. I'd estimate that, on average, we get 30 to 50 of those photos used in one form or another by large and small papers and magazines. That's a pretty amazing return on a $200 investment, don't you think? The attached samples are not new, they are variations of ads we've all seen many times. I recommend you start clipping ads for and write ups about concerts starting today. Collect them in a folder over the next few months, then use the photo to work backwards when in comes time to create your own ads.

January 30, 1997

S. Zeke Orlinsky
Patuxent Publishing Group
10750 Patuxent Park-way
Columbia, NM 21044

Dear Mr. Orlinsky,

We've just signed Ray Charles to present a concert to benefit The Maryland School for the Blind at The Meyerhoff Symphony on June 20, 1997. Governor and Mrs. Glendening have agreed to be our Honorary Chairs and Smith, Sommerville & Case have signed on as our major sponsors.

I'm writing to ask that Patuxent Publishing Group act as one of our media sponsors. Your participation would help make this first concert the major success it can be. I would certainly make sure that you are listed in all brochures, ads, posters and the concert program. I would also include a full page advertisement in our program and send along tickets for our pre concert VIP Champagne Reception at The Meyerhoff.

I've asked WJZ-TV and The Baltimore Sun to also serve as media sponsors but I believe your audience is unique and especially loyal. Your support would make a real difference. Please let me know if I can answer any questions.

Yours,

Jim Hollan
Director of Development

Smith, Somerville & Case, LLC.
presents

June 20, 1997 In a concert to benefit The Maryland School for the Blind

Ray Charles

Fax

From: Jim Hollan
              The Maryland School for the Blind
              3501 Taylor Avenue
              Baltimore, Maryland 21236-4499
              410/444-5000 ext.288
              410/426-2590

To: Sylvia XXXXX
              XXXXXXXXXX
              XXXXXXXXXX

Dear Sylvia,

I've got Ray Charles and the entire stage Band with Rayletts at The Meyerhoff on Friday June 20, 1997 8:OOPM tickets $18.50, $27.50 and $36.00 through Box Office at 410/783-8000. Opening act is Baltimore's own Deanna Bogart.

Governor and Mrs. Glendening are honorary chairs and Smith, Sommerville and Case are the major sponsor of this concert. Proceeds to benefit The Maryland School for the Blind which is a private, non profit organization serving blind and visually impaired children state wide since 1853.

Also have $125 VIP Seat and Reception at 6:30 prior to concert with catering by Spike and Charlie's and introduction of wine with brailled labels from Chauptier in the Rhone Valley which will get some coverage from Wine Spectator! Celebs accepting already range from Tippy Martinez to Mike Miller, Mayor Schmoke, spattering of other congressional types. This event will simply be flat if you don't agree to bring a guest and come to the VIP reception! Say Yes Sylvia...... We love you.

Jim

The Window

The Maryland School for the Blind   •   Baltimore, Maryland   •   Spring 1997

The Ray Charles Concert to Benefit The Maryland School for the Blind!

Get ready to have your socks knocked off on Friday, June 20 at 8 p.m., when the legendary Ray Charles gives a concert to benefit The Maryland School for the Blind at the Meyerhoff Symphony Hall in Baltimore! Governor and Mrs. Parris Glendening are the honorary chairs for this extraordinary night of music presented by the prestigious law firm of Smith, Somerville & Case, L.L.C.

For more than 40 years, Ray Charles has been dazzling audiences around the world. He is a 12-time Grammy Award winner and received a star on Hollywood Boulevard's "Walk of Fame" in 1981 in recognition of both his artistic and humanitarian achievements. In 1993, Ray Charles received the National Medal of Arts presented by President Bill Clinton and in 1994 he received The World Music Award in Monte Carlo for his "Lifelong Contribution to the Music Industry." Ray Charles truly is a national treasure and an international phenomenon.

The concert promises to be a fun-filled, foot stomping, hand clapping night to remember. All proceeds will benefit The Maryland School for the Blind and help further the school's goal to provide the best possible education and learning experiences for children in Maryland who are blind and visually impaired.

As if Ray Charles were not enough. The evening will start with the explosive talent of Deanna Bogart — described by *Down Beat* magazine as "an extravagant entertainer." A local talent and winner of 11 Washington Area Music Awards, the release of her most recent album — "New Address," has moved her

more and more onto the large national stage.

Tickets are on sale at the Meyerhoff ticket box office as of May 1st. We urge you to purchase — we're expecting a sell out! Special V.I.P. tickets, including a pre-show champagne reception and preferred seating, are available for $125 each.

"The Ray Charles concert is a major event that we hope will take the school to a new level. With the support of our many friends, we hope this concert will mark the beginning of a new tradition at MSB, an annual concert that will be a major fundraiser and a major friend raiser," said Jim Hollan, MSB Development Director. If this concert is to be a success, we need your help.

Ticket Prices

$18.50 .... Terrace

$27.50 .... Upper Orchestra

$35.00 ..... Grand Tier Orchestra

$125.00 .... V.I.P. Seating
(includes pre-concert reception & preferred seat)

Order Today!
Meyerhoff Symphony Hall
1212 Cathedral St., Balto., MD 21201
(410) 783-8000

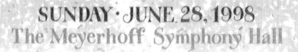

Chapter 8
The Program

After the main ad and the adverting plan is put together, I go to work on the program. You must *always* have a program. It is a thank you to your contributors, a chance to tell the story of your organization to the audience and it is an extraordinarily effective tool for selling your next concert. It is so important that I often stretch the budget to make the program as handsome as possible.

I've used sample pages from a program here but you should notice certain key elements. The cover features the performer and your organization. Sometimes it will also feature the major sponsor as in the case of "Smith, Somerville & Case present Ray Charles." The title page *always* features the major sponsors and I will tell you that time after time many of these sponsors have told me how impressed they are to see their name linked with major celebrities. It is not an everyday event for even some of the largest sponsors and they often ask for extra copies of the program just like any other fan.

I regularly approach major political figures to send a photo and write an endorsement. Actually I write a sample endorsement for them and nine times out of ten I get almost exactly the same words back. I believe there is a certain panache added to your program when the major political representatives in your state are shown to be in agreement about the good work of your organization. It adds another layer of importance to your event.

Early on in your program should be a write up of your host for the evening and, as you can see in the sample page for our Mistress of Ceremonies, I take advantage of some extra space to use a picture of the students we serve. This is also an opportunity to talk about your organization and your cause as you can see from the attached samples about The Maryland School for the Blind. Remember that this is a chance to tell your story in an interesting way. It is not the appropriate time to delve into a 50-page discourse. As a rule of thumb I limit this section to no more than two pages.

The largest number of pages are dedicated to sponsors. As you may remember from an earlier chapter, we have full-page and half-page advertisements pledged to our silver and gold sponsors. I often give a half-page ad to those people who donate important services. On one you will see an ad for Mort Kuff who donated the graphic design and poster for The Smothers Brothers Concert and another ad for Tammy Hoffer who donated her time and film as the pre-concert and after-concert photographer for this same event. It was a very inexpensive way for me to thank two great artists for their very valuable contributions.

I've dabbled with just selling ads in our program but I personally never had very much success. It may work for some but it has never been an efficient use of my time. I try to use the space in different ways, focusing on selling sponsorships rather than ads. I also thank the sponsors in other sections where they are listed by category and on occasion they will be mentioned in some copy. It's just fine to thank people more than once.

Smith, Somerville & Case, L.L.C.

Presents

Ray Charles

in a concert to benefit

The Maryland School for the Blind

welcomed by

WMAR-TV, Patuxent Publishing Co., The New Daily Record, Edgemark Systems & BGE

Table of Contents

Thank you for coming.
Enjoy the Show!

STATE OF MARYLAND
OFFICE OF THE GOVERNOR

Dear Friends:

The Maryland School for the Blind is a nationally recognized leader in providing services for the blind, visually impaired and multi-disabled students. The school did not earn this reputation without a great deal of support from the community, the State and its dedicated teachers.

As Honorary Co-Chairs of the Ray Charles Concert, Frances Anne and I want to salute the Maryland School for the Blind for 144 years of service. This school not only serves the blind and visually impaired, it serves all of Maryland's citizens. Because the school is a model demonstration site for the education and employment of individuals with visual impairment, Maryland businesses can look to the Maryland School for the Blind for qualified employees. Maryland needs an educated and trained workforce, and because of your dedication to providing education and Skills for Independence, your students are ready to take their place in the workplace of the 21st century.

You are to be congratulated on producing this fine event. May this evening be a tribute to your success in demonstrating that the visually impaired are a valuable resource to their community. We applaud the Maryland School for the Blind -- staff, teachers, parents and students.

Sincerely,

Parris N. Glendening
Governor

Frances Hughes Glendening
First Lady

UNITED STATES SENATE
WASHINGTON, D. C. 20510

It is my pleasure to congratulate The Maryland School For The Blind for 144 years of dedicated service to the children of Maryland.

Since its beginning, The Maryland School For The Blind has maintained a reputation for excellence and innovation. For this reason, children in the State of Maryland that are blind and/or visually impaired can function effectively in society.

I applaud The Maryland School For The Blind on its achievements and commitment to the children. You have truly made a difference in the lives you touched and the environment they live in.

I hope everyone enjoys the concert! As always, I remain,

Sincerely,

Barbara A. Mikulski,
United States Senator

SENATE OF MARYLAND
ANNAPOLIS, MARYLAND 21401-1991

It is truly an honor for me to be included as part of this exciting event that will support the Maryland School for the Blind.

I would like to take this opportunity to commend the Maryland School for the Blind for all of its efforts on behalf of blind and visually impaired students since 1853. Your commitment to excellence has not gone unnoticed and many people from Maryland have benefitted from your hard work and dedication.

Please extend my best wishes for a successful event and continued success in all your future endeavors on behalf of the blind and visually impaired citizens in the state of Maryland.

Sincerely,

Thomas V. Mike Miller, Jr.

Mistress of Ceremonies

Mary Beth Marsden is co-anchor of NewsChannel 2 *First at Five* and NewsChannel 2 *Nightside at 11* with Stan Stovall. She has been a member of the NewsChannel 2 team since May 1988. Mary Beth came to WMAR-TV from WNEP-TV in Scranton, Pennsylvania.

Since coming to Baltimore, Mary Beth has become very active in the community. In addition to speaking to local schools and businesses, she lends ongoing support to the Johns Hopkins Children's Center, People's Homesteading Group and the Baltimore Zoo.

A graduate of the University of Maryland, Mary Beth received her B.A. Degree in Radio, Television and Film. She's a Maryland native and currently lives with her husband, Mark McGrath, in Baltimore.

Linda Reynolds and Joshua Gregory

❖*Special Thanks*

Behind the Scenes Superstars:
Wendy Blair
C. Prevost Boyce
Raleigh Brent
Eddie Castellano
Joe Chin
Jim Datovech
Glenn DiChiera
W. Gary Dorsch
Dottie Doub
Dennis Edelstein
Dave Evans
Nikki Gary
Lori Grant
Mary Harrington
Bill Hebrank
Norence Hinson
Mort Kuff
Lindenmeyer Munroe
Dave Linthicum
John Peltz
Janet Praid
Burt Richwien
Marge Saunders
Pam Schirmer
JoAnn Trumbule
Thomas W. Valenti
Maria Velleggia
W. Mike Walsh
Cheryl Ware
Rosaria Wolff

Stage Manager & Production:
McShane Glover
Noteworthy Productions

Catering:
Spike & Charlie's

Official Photographer:
Tammy Hoffer

Program Editor:
Sherry Thompson

Printing:
David Stevenson
Printing Corporation of America

Meyerhoff:
Gabe Purviance
Kathy Marciano
Ennis Seibert
Chris Drolsum
Local #19, IATSE

An event like this cannot happen if not for the cooperation and support of many people. I've tried to name all of you and I apologize for any omissions or errors. A very special note of thanks to those individuals who gave their time, talent and energy to help make tonight's concert a reality. These are the silent superstars who work behind the scences. Thank you all for going that extra mile for a great cause.

Jim Hollan
Director of Development

"See you all next year!"

24

Chapter 9
The VIP Reception and the Meet and Greet

You might think it odd that the VIP reception and the meet and greet merit their own chapter but I can't emphasize enough just how important they are. This is where you make the real money in an event and it should not be overlooked or under developed. Far too often I've seen a missed opportunity at this key event or noticed that there was no VIP event at all.

The VIP reception is a "special" event for your "special" supporters. It is not about value for money or including all the little folks you want to thank for their on-going support. It is a blatant attempt to cater to the "just like the neighbor next door" syndrome that affects so many of us. The VIP reception clearly marks out those people who are part of the "in crowd," the *sanctum sanctorum*, the folks on the red carpet as opposed to those behind the ropes. For something like the Academy Awards, you earn your spot on that red carpet by talent or long-term production credits. For an event like this you can simply buy your way in. It's so much more American.

Don't cheat your VIPs. Make your event so special that they are not only glad they came, they will definitely come again next year. This is a chance to thank your major donors and charm potential major donors for next year. It is an opportunity to recruit potential board members and potential new donors, and to network with local government leaders.

I make a point of having some VIPs at my VIP reception. By that I mean that I invite celebrities who will be recognized by the other guests. I can generally locate a few political, sports and entertainment personalities in our area to come for the reception even if they must leave for the concert. Their presence adds a certain panache to the event. People like to go to work the next day and say how they were chatting with "The Mayor" or "The Governor" or "The Senator" last night. Time after time, I've had major money people who might be otherwise unimpressed with wealth or politics ask if I could introduce them to a sports celebrity at an event. One of my hard to impress major donors was overjoyed at the opportunity to meet some of the Baltimore Orioles he had grown up admiring as a boy. When I suggested we get some photos of him standing with his heroes he all but kissed me. I'd found a way to impress and thank my donor that he would never forget. In the bargain my friends from the Orioles enjoyed knowing that they could help my cause simply by their presence. Another one of those famous win-win situations.

The feature performer sometimes appears at this event but that is not usual. They are often busy with preparation and pre-show nerves; moreover, the feature performer usually likes the evening to build towards their appearance on stage.

I often ask a local television celebrity to act as our master of ceremonies and I always ask that they come for the reception. You would be amazed how many people feel that the local news anchor or weather man is someone they already know, since they see them every night. Once again your VIPs are reminded that this is a very special event and they are part of the "in crowd." Asking local celebrities to add their presence to your VIP event is not very difficult but it requires some planning ahead of time. Make sure you invite the celebrity and their "guest" to be your guests, and treat them like the royalty they are. They understand their role and they will be pleased to have their photo taken with your other guests. Make sure that you have a few people available for introductions and make sure you have a least one photographer for the entire reception.

My preference for a reception is heavy hor d'ouevers. This is not meant to be a dinner but I don't want it to be skimpy either. I like the food to be available at several stations and I also like some items to be passed by waitstaff on trays as guests chat. I abhor lines for food and I hate food items that require a plate, fork, cutting and balancing. The food should be clever, different, easy to pick from a plate and beautifully displayed. To that end, I generally locate very *nouvelle* caterers for my events. I want most of my guests to see things for the first time. I want them to feel that *everything* about my concert was special, right down to the food served at the reception. I go to restaurants that are on the cutting edge and talk to them about putting on a class presentation for a very upscale clientele. I ask them to produce a quality event at a reasonable cost. I also point out that this is a chance to display their creativity for people who are willing to pay $125 a ticket for a private reception — in other words, people who are likely to employ upscale caterers. This is definitely a chance to move away from the standard catering so boringly familiar to everyone. Why start your evening with a statement that says "This is the same old stuff" when you have the chance to say "This is top of the line and this is something new."

After a few start-up years of very low key catering for the VIP reception, The Cystic Fibrosis Foundation of Maryland got the Maryland Chefs association to adopt this event as their charity and they donate their services for the reception. This reception has grown to a spectacular event in its own right drawing 750 people to a feast prepared by 20 or so of Maryland's top restaurants and chefs. Needless to say that would be an excellent thing to do if you can pull it off.

I almost always pay for the catering but I usually get the alcohol donated for free. I usually have wine, beer, soda and mineral water at my receptions. I don't think mixed drinks are necessary and I've bumped into very few complaints over the years. I generally go to a liquor distributor and ask if one of their brands would be willing to donate the wine and beer. All liquor companies have promotional budgets from each of their accounts and they are often willing to donate several cases of product. I usually offer to feature the distributor as a silver sponsor, give them a half page ad in the program and four tickets to the VIP concert. The savings can be several thousand dollars and the rewards can be surprising. When we found out that M. Chapoutier, one of the great wine producers in France, was manufacturing a braille wine label, we contacted the distributor, who contacted the importer, who contacted M.

Chapoutier to ask if he would sponsor The Ray Charles Concert to benefit The Maryland School for the Blind. Do you see the connection? Well he did and he arranged for the wine to be introduced in the United States at our concert; moreover, he autographed an over-sized bottle as a special presentation to Ray Charles. Guess what? He was also a big Ray Charles fan.

The wines were spectacular, many of my blind VIPs were knocked out by the concept of brailled wine labels, and we had photos published nationally in publications as diverse as *Wine Spectator* and *The Beverage Journal* because of the unique spin. It took paying attention, asking around and jumping at an opportunity, but we came up with even another *special* spin on our inaugural event. Most producers are proud of their product and often pleased to donate it for a worthwhile cause. As a footnote, make sure that you have the donation processed correctly through a distributor so that state liquor laws are not accidentally violated.

You want to have the VIP reception close by your concert area. Many concert halls have a place for just such an event, but others don't. When your venue has no place for your reception you should do a quick survey in a block or two radius of the venue. I've had a small museum open its doors for a small fee. I mentioned the Governor's yacht loaned for an event close by the water and we've had a nearby restaurant give us space since they were going to cater. Some events become so big that they outgrow the venue. In this case you may pay to have tents erected next to the concert hall. You can afford to do that when you have many hundreds of VIPs since you are already dealing with a substantial bonus income. Use your imagination. Make it special. These are your most generous supporters.

I generally schedule the reception for one and a half hours before the concert. For an eight o'clock concert the reception should start at 6:30. Close the bars down at 7:45 and start moving your guests into the concert hall. I find a longer amount of time gains very little except tired guests and a few additional drunks. I find an hour is too short except for a very small event.

It is important that you go to several of these events yourself in order to get a sense as to what works and what doesn't. In particular, try to go to one or two at the same venue you plan to use. No charity is going to turn down anyone willing to spend the dollars to come to their VIP reception. If your organization thinks it unseemly to pay for you to go to such a classy event ask them how on earth they expect you to get people to come to your event if you don't know what the standard is. As an aside, I would also recommend you start looking for a new position because you are working for a bunch of cheap skates and they will never really get it.

Let me pause for a moment and run through a list of stupid things I've seen at VIP events.

- Running out of wine 30 minutes into a 90-minute reception!!!
- Having food stations carve and serve food items. This requires people to line up and wait and wait and wait as they get more and more annoyed.
- Serving big, sloppy, saucy food items that are impossible to eat without covering yourself in sauce.
- Serving the standard pre-frozen, no flavor, mini desserts that can now be purchased at any major Ernie's House of Discount Frozen Food.
- Holding a reception in a space that is much too big. A too large space will make your group seem very small and unimportant.
- Holding a reception in a space that is too small. Nobody wants to stand shoulder to shoulder in a pack. Don't allow your reception to become overcrowded in order to milk a few more dollars out of your crowd. Nothing insures success for future events like a sellout. Don't be afraid to say "I'm sorry, but we've sold out." Conversely, an overcrowded, unpleasant reception is the kiss of death for next year's event.
- Creating a bottle neck at the very beginning of your event by having only one or two people check in your guests when you should have six or eight.
- Failing to make this "special" event "special."

The bottom line is that your VIPs must feel they received VIP treatment. The best food, elegant service, rubbing elbows with other important people, the best seating and a sense that they are fundamental to the success of your event. This is a chance for many of your guests to shine in the eyes of their loved ones. Their spouse is not likely to be all that impressed by an important board meeting or power lunch but they can be impressed by attending this special evening. Make your VIPs feel even more important in the eyes of their spouse or guests and they will be back year after year. Everybody wants to feel important. Make sure your CEO and Board Chair are mixing and networking with all the VIPs as you thank everyone for their support.

The VVIPs, that would be the *Very* Very Important People get invited to a "meet and greet" with the stars of the evening. This event is almost always held just after the concert and involves very few people. In my experience the number falls somewhere around 50 people including the feature act. In this age of drunk driving awareness I generally serve coffee, mineral water and some sort of very special dessert.

Most venues have a green room designed specifically for this event. If not, I use a dressing room near the star's dressing room. Once again keep it special and upscale. Make sure the food/coffee set up is elegant, this is not the place for paper cups. Make sure you have wait staff pouring the coffee and keeping the desserts properly displayed. Make sure that your photographer has plenty of film and make sure that *every* guest at this reception has a small group photo with the star. My favorite photo for this event is of the star, a major donor with spouse or guest and your organization's CEO. If you have four people from an organization then the photo becomes six people instead of four.

The feature act needs 10 or 15 minutes to change and relax after the show and they will sometimes have an acquaintance or two stop by to say hello. The performer rarely spends more than 20 minutes or so at the meet and greet but that is plenty of time for them to mix, have their photo taken with everyone, and graciously be on their way. Your guests will likely linger another 10 or 15 minutes, then you should start moving them out. I schedule the event for immediately after the concert. In order to make your meet and greet secure from fans seeking autographs or a word with the star, you must have security prohibiting access to backstage and security at the door of the Green Room reception area. A backstage pass for your meet and greet guests is not only an aid to security it makes for a lovely take home memento.

Start the meet and greet just after the concert, that gives you about 10 or 15 minutes for your guests to arrive and chat before the star shows up, about 20 to 25 minutes for your star to mix and another 10 to 15 minutes for your group to say their good nights. Your timeline is 40 to 50 minutes but it should be the most fruitful part of the evening. It is a time to pass along congratulations for a wonderful concert; a wonderful reception, a delightful evening all in all. Everyone goes home feeling great.

Starting at the end, let's work backwards as we look at ways to maximize the benefits of these two reception events. Within a few short days after the concert, I have two copies of every group photo taken at the meet and greet. I generally get 5 X 7s and I purchase nice frames with a volume discount, not great frames but definitely not cheap frames. I call each of my major donors and make an appointment to drop by with their photos from the concert. Everyone wants to see me! Actually everyone wants to see their photo with the major performer, but I don't have a big ego and I take it that they really want to see me.

Why frame two photos? One for home and one for the office. All year long your sponsor gets to show off that photo with Ray Charles or some other superstar as they reflect positively on your special event. I use this delivery of the photos as an opportunity to make sure that they are committed as sponsors for the following year and I often ask for their help in getting some of their friends involved in next year's event as new sponsors. Over the years, the vast majority of these conversations center around whom next year's performer is going to be; we rarely discuss whether or not they are returning as a sponsor, that's usually a given.

It is often the case that my major sponsors bring one of their very important clients to the meet and greet as a guest. If that is the case, I always make an additional copy of the framed photo. I want my sponsor happy and I've had reasonable success over the years turning some of these guests of sponsors into sponsors. You can't imagine how happy I am when I walk into a sponsor's office and see several of my photos on their wall.

My major sponsor gets several framed photos for their friends or family. I also bring a major presentation piece if available such as a handsomely framed and autographed poster. I've seen some of these gifts displayed in the lobby of major corporations that are proud of their sponsorship and their association with major performers. Once again it is a situation where everyone wins.

Key photos with the performer are sent out to the local press with a release describing the event and announcing the dollars

raised. This follow-up promotion is valuable in its own right and sets the stage for next year's event.

I do something very similar with the many photos I've taken at the VIP reception. In particular we sort out photos of guests with VIPs. I usually send a 5x7 in a nice cardboard folder along with a personal thank you note. For VIPs whom I sense we may move up to the sponsor level, I again make a point of delivering the photos personally. It is a lovely opportunity to talk about sponsorship.

The VIP reception and the meet and greet are the ultimate networking opportunity for your organization. This is a golden opportunity for you, your CEO and key board members to "get to know" potential supporters. ABC corporation may have signed on as a sponsor because they are crazy about Ray Charles; however, you now have a golden opportunity to develop ABC as a "friend of your organization."

Since the VIP reception is an event within an event, it is also an excellent opportunity for a separate sponsorship. On occasion,

I've been to events where the sponsor not only paid for the reception but included nicely wrapped gifts featuring their products. It was a bonus for our VIPs and another "special" touch for our special event. Remember to treat this as an opportunity to thank your very best supporters and you will come along just fine. Properly managed, the VIP event will drive all of your major sponsorships over the course of a few years.

Backstage Pass

After Show Reception

Second Annual Concert for The MD School for the Blind

Chapter 10
Putting It All Together

Now that you have a basic outline of the entire process, let's go back to our original rough budget, sharpen our pencils and decide whether or not we are going to move ahead with our concert. That first budget kept our expenses fairly flat and we built in a contingency expense that projected a total cost that we will round up to $81,000. We should be able to bring our concert, with all advertising, receptions and even the framed follow-up photos in for less than this amount if we are conscientious. We estimated that our income from ticket sales would come in a little over $83,000. In other words we are basically at a break-even on the concert based on projected ticket sales.

In preliminary meetings with my planning committee we estimated that we could raise at least $50,000 in sponsorships. Since some of my likely sponsors serve on this committee, I believe this is a reasonable estimate and it means we are projecting a $50,000 profit the very first year out; nevertheless, this is the time for us to stop and reevaluate our goals and ask ourselves some hard questions. Since we are about to make a major commitment of time, energy and dollars we need to define our goals so that we have some way of evaluating our success.

Is the goal of this concert to maximize income? No. The fact is that we could probably raise close to the same amount of net dollars if we had no event at all and just relied on our key sponsors to make contributions. That at least would be the case for this year, but our long-term goal is to grow the concert to include more sponsors and higher levels of sponsorship. We are focusing on the *development* part of Development. We are going to build up our income over a period of time, *develop* our resources so that the same kind of event raises more net dollars each year. Remember The Hard Travelers in our first chapter? They started with a modest net profit and spent years *developing* that event into the tremendous success it would become. They also had a great time in the process. Fund raising is often a one time action; however, development, by definition, is a long-term growth process. I belong to the National Society of Fund Raising Executives; however, most people in my field are called "development" officers. There is a distinction and one worth thinking about. Relative to this concert we are willing to put in more time and take more risk because we are not focusing on the short-term gain but *developing* a source of long-term growth dollars. This investment in our future is like planting a garden for the first time. The work is actually harder the first year out: we have to break up the ground, plan where things will go, work tough soil, hope that our garden notes are correct relative to our unique area and make lots of first-time investments, all with little hands-on experience. Next year we will work with soil already in better shape, we will build on our success and correct our errors. We will know better what works and what doesn't. We will likely put in a similar amount of work for a much more abundant return. Several years down the road we will likely put in less work for a truly abundant return as we learn all the ins and outs, the tricks of the trade that work in our garden. To totally beat this extended metaphor to death, we are groundbreaking and that is always the most difficult phase of planning and planting. (I have no idea where this garden metaphor came from since I grew up in Manhattan and thought food grew naturally in cans.)

Is this concert about more than money? Absolutely. We are going into this event with the hope that we will gain name recognition for our organization as well as positive publicity about our mission. We hope to involve some corporations that have not yet become part of our donor family. We hope to use this event to *develop*, there's that word again, new friendships with the guests and friends of sponsors. We hope to *develop* more recognition with some of our state political leaders who should be in attendance and we hope to excite some of our own board members who have been in a rut these last few years relative to what we do as an organization. We are reaching out in a very public way to *develop* new friends.

If we keep these various goals in mind we will likely avoid some typical first time mistakes. In particular, by focusing more on the long-term development, we will invest some of our dollars in the future rather than choosing to maximize profits in year one. What do I mean by that? If your first-year event is not special you may not get a chance for a second-year event or you will have a difficult time convincing sponsors to come back for another "barely adequate" and "not very satisfying" event. Keep the "special" in your special event. Have a beautiful program for everyone entering the concert hall so that your sponsors are proud to see their company listed in a first-rate publication. It doesn't hurt that some of your non sponsors feel a bit left out by not seeing their company listed. It doesn't hurt that your half-page sponsors are glad to be involved so prominently but a little jealous that they are not as prominent as the full-page ads. If the governor is there and the mayor and several other big shots it is a motivator for your half-page sponsor to move up to a full-page next year. People want to be in the top echelon if they feel the top echelon is actually a special place to be. Perhaps the greatest single motivator I've seen to move sponsors up the ladder of sponsorship is watching members of the higher tiers get invited to something they don't normally get invited to do. It's a socially competitive world out there and we might as well use it to our advantage.

Armed with a general sense that we can make a profit on this event, a belief that we can grow this event over the years and a belief that we can, as a bonus, greatly enhance our public image in a positive way, we decided to move forward with this first annual concert fundraiser for our cause.

In the case of the Ray Charles concert we went to the board of directors at the school and presented our plan. The basic concept of a major annual concert had been approved many months before and I now needed to present our projected budget and a fairly detailed outline of our event for approval. It's one thing approving the development of a plan; quite another to commit to an actual event that is likely to cost in the range of $80,000. I also knew that some members of the board didn't buy into this idea at all. They thought it far too risky and felt it to be much too much of a reach for our organization. Some of this worry was legitimate but a goodly bit also reflected a ". . . we haven't done this before; therefore, we like-ly won't be able to do it" mentality. I was committed to this plan as were the members of my committee but we knew our board of directors were nervous. To their credit, the board voted to move ahead with the concert even though it would be a substantial finan-cial commitment and many were clearly nervous. The nervousness was quickly dispersed when Mike Kelly, one of the board members, raised his hand just after the vote to move ahead was taken. "Mr. Chairman," he said, "I'm proud to say that my law firm, Smith, Somerville and Case, would be proud to act as the major sponsor for this event." Before the meeting was over, two other board members pledged their firms to Gold level sponsorships. I left the meeting with permission to move ahead and $35,000 in sponsorships!

We moved forward immediately to tie down our venue and performer dates and immediately ran into some problems. The dates Ray was available had changed once again and we were forced into a series of phone calls back and forth across the country between the agency in California, the venue in Baltimore and my office at the school. After two weeks and perhaps 60 calls, along with several bottles of Mylanta, we tied down a Friday night in June. There are always exceptions, but as a general rule Fridays and Saturdays are always the easiest nights to sell tickets. Sundays are next but start your concert an hour earlier, 7 P.M. rather than 8 P.M. so that folks don't worry about a late night before Monday work. It is hardest to get people to come out for a show on Monday, slightly easier on Tuesday, then Wednesday, and easier still on Thursday. You might as well factor in as many easy steps as possible and I pre-fer weekends when I can get them. I have made exceptions several times when I was able to get a performer in my area between con-certs. If you have a major act in Richmond, Virginia on one weekend and Philadelphia the following weekend you can often arrange for a substantial discount if you book them mid-week between venues. Everybody wins on that one.

Our contract with the performer contained a typical clause that he will not perform within the Baltimore Metropolitan area for six months prior to our concert. Nothing takes the wind out of your sails more than having your special artist do a show in your area a month before your concert. Your "special" event is no longer special and general ticket sales suffer. Artists are generally prepared to agree to this type of stipulation.

With a performer, a venue and a performance date tied down, we went in search of an opening act. Ray has a road show that is 70 minutes long and that is not long enough for a concert evening. We want an opening act that is compatible with Ray's show and one that will last about 30 to 40 minutes. Ray, in fact, has the right to approve the opening act written into his contract. This is not uncommon, as professionals do not want poor quality acts to open for them.

The joy of having a famous performer and a great concert hall is that you can negotiate with acts on the way up. We thought of several appropriate artists in the Baltimore/Washington area and settled on Deanna Bogart. She was a rock and roll/boogie woogie pianist, vocalist and saxophone player with a dynamite backup band. She had just released her third album and was just ready to break out onto the national scene. Under normal circumstances Deanna would have charged several thousand dollars for a performance, but she was really excited to open for the great Ray Charles. She was also delighted to play at The Meyerhoff Symphony Hall. We agreed on a price of $600 and a dozen complimentary tickets. I also promised to introduce her to Ray! Once again everyone was happy.

I've certainly asked for my share of support for acts like Sissy and her Amazing Cats or the Small Town Vocal Arts Society. Potential sponsors usually look blank or offer a minimal amount of support. They hear small time and they think small time. The entire experience is altogether different when you have a major performer like Ray Charles. Potential sponsors hear big time and they think big time. The fact that we had a major law firm as our banner sponsor was also significant. Potential sponsors recognized that we were putting on a top-notch event and they responded appropriately.

The day after receiving authorization from our board to move forward and picking up our major sponsor, we sent a letter to the governor of our state and his wife to act as honorary chairs for this concert. We thought they would add prestige and clout to this event. As it was also our goal to make ourselves more visible to the governor this seemed a perfect opportunity. Several weeks before, I had called the governor's appointments secretary to ask about the process. They asked a few questions and suggested I write a letter outlining the event once I knew we were moving forward. I've attached a copy of that letter.

January 4, 1996

JoAnn Trumbule
Director of Scheduling and Public Relations
State House
Annapolis, Maryland 21401

Dear JoAnn,

The Maryland School for the Blind has provided uninterrupted service to blind and
visually impaired children in Maryland since 1853. We are a private, nonprofit
organization serving every school district in the state. We provide outreach services for
students who are "just blind" so that they can stay in their local schools and we have a
residential program in Baltimore for blind students with multiple disabilities.

This year we will present the first annual concert to benefit The Maryland School
for the Blind featuring Ray Charles at Pier Six in Baltimore. We are still negotiating the
exact date but we expect it to be in July 1996 and I'm glad to report that the law firm of
Smith, Sommerville and Case has already agreed to be our major sponsor.

This event is meant to raise a significant amount of money but it is also designed to
get our school better known throughout the state. I'm writing to ask that Governor and
Mrs. Glendening lend their name to this event by serving as Honorary Chairs. Their
recognition of our long term commitment to blind and visually impaired children including
those with multiple disabilities would be of enormous benefit.

I've enclosed our current annual report which gives a bit more information about
our history and I stand ready to answer any questions you may have. As a footnote I
should add that our school president, Lou Tutt, just received a national award from The
Council of Schools for the Blind which represents schools for the Blind nationwide. The
award, only the fifth one ever given, recognizes his leadership and contributions to the
field of blindness and visual impairment. The governor has every reason to be proud of
The Maryland School for the Blind.

Yours,

Jim Hollan
Director of Development

It's very nice to have one of the wealthiest people in the area act as your honorary chair but it is often difficult to get that person to accept the position. I'm giving away one of my trade secrets, but I've found the governors of many states are very generous with their time for a worthy cause. They are usually more generous with larger events in prestigious settings. You might not have a lot of luck getting the governor to act as chair for The Epping Forest Accordian Association Annual Spam Festival but your chances increase as you move up the social scale. Putting a few thousand people together in one spot is also helpful.

We had one or two committee members wonder if it was appropriate to have the Democratic governor as chair. "Wouldn't that alienate the Republicans?" they asked. I believe that you invite the *governor*, the elected leader of your state. The party doesn't matter. You may put off a few people who think the governor is awful wherever you are; however, the reputation of any state governor adds amazing clout to your event. In our case, the governor agreed within two weeks and we were able to approach potential sponsors with a package that included Ray Charles, a major Baltimore law firm, the finest concert hall in the state and the governor as our honorary chairman. With that combination a lot more people gave us a careful hearing. I also used that combination to approach potential sponsors with whom I did not have a relationship or personal contact.

As we worked on dollar sponsors we also went in search of media sponsors. In general the media give you advertising space instead of dollars but the advertising is the backbone of ticket sales so it does have great value. We want to develop a sense of celebrity and we want to have regular news coverage of our event since we believe that every positive showing of our name benefits our organization. Remember, we were considered "invisible" going into this process and positive public recognition is one of our goals.

Our first step was to approach major print media in our area asking for sponsorship. We took our regular sponsor levels and doubled the dollar rates for appropriate media sponsor levels. In other words $10,000 of advertising would qualify as a Gold Sponsor rather than $5,000 cash. Any media representative worth their salt will tell you that it is fairly easy to get a paper to sponsor your event if you are a major advertiser. The classic right hand washing the left. In our case we did no advertising whatsoever; and we really had no major board contacts who were major print advertisers; consequently, we had to do a lot of cold calling. The major paper in our area turned us down but Patuxent Publishing, a publisher of 13 regional newspapers agreed to sign on. They would run three separate 1/4 page ads in all of their papers but vary the dates so that we had various levels of coverage starting about 10 weeks before our concert. We also had some success with a few regional papers that agreed to run an ad or two but would not commit to a sponsorship. We received an ad commitment from *The Daily Record*. This is a small-circulation paper but it is directed at the local business and legal community. Although the circulation was small, many of our sponsors read this paper and we wanted them to see their event getting regular promotion. Picking up sponsorships, including media, is especially difficult the first year out. We had hoped for more print media sponsorship but we were satisfied with what we obtained.

Signing on our television sponsor turned out to be a snap. We approached the station with a cover letter asking for sponsorship and asking them to develop a TV ad for our concert and on-air support. We also asked that they provide the master of ceremonies if the station signed on. Our first choice was the evening news anchorwoman, Mary Beth Marsden. We exchanged a few phone calls with the station and received a "Yes" in less than a month. Unlike print media, you usually obtain only one TV and one radio station as a major media sponsor.

The radio stations were quite another matter. Several stations were interested in being sponsors but they had a tiny audience and several larger stations would sponsor but only give us limited coverage and they wanted a lot in return. We decided to say "No" to the big ones and worked out a deal with several of the smaller stations where we supplied tickets as prizes for contests in the weeks before the concert. At a combined cost of 60 of our cheapest tickets we insured some radio coverage in the weeks leading up to the concert.

Media sponsorship deals primarily with advertising, but you will also get substantial free press coverage if you carefully plan a program of press releases. Your campaign should start at least three and often four or five months before your event. For this concert we had a master press contact list of approximately 300 news outlets in the Maryland, Virginia and District of Columbia area as well as the near parts of Pennsylvania. From newspapers to newsletters we targeted three major press releases. The 50 largest markets also received photos with their release. These photos are normally purchased at a minimal fee from the promotional representative of the major act. In this case the photos turned out to be a major source of irritation as we could rarely get the promoter to respond to our repeated inquiries. We also make a point of getting on every entertainment "calendar" we can. These are the "What's happening this weekend" parts of papers and they require planning as you must get your notice in at least a month and often two months ahead of time. Also remember that different sections of major papers have different editors and you need to approach them separately. We produce generic press releases for each of the major three mailings but we try to personalize with a separate note whenever possible. These feature pieces can have a significant impact on the success of your event. They don't happen by accident and I advice you to target your PR campaign early on.

We actually have one additional type of sponsor that we've not mentioned yet. I usually work to get certain services donated and offer a sponsorship in return. In this case a photographer who frequently worked on our annual report volunteered her time for the pre-concert reception and the after-concert meet and greet. She also donated all the film. A savings for me of $500 to $1,000. I offered two VIP tickets and a half-page ad in our program as a trade and we all came away happy. I usually get the artwork, a generic ad, a poster and program cover donated by a graphic artist in return for a half-page ad and a few VIP tickets. Very good artists usually want to see their work presented in a very professional way and are willing to donate their art as a portfolio builder. I have friends in Washington who usually get major ad agencies to donate the entire ad campaign. The agency wants the freedom to create an exciting campaign which they often enter in professional contests. They don't often get this kind of freedom from big-budget clients worried about the subtle risks of demographic changes. It's a win-win for everyone.

As you can see, we are finding ways to chip away at the numbers built into our budget and that is the way I prefer to go. I want to budget an expense and hope to eliminate or lower it, rather than just assume I will get tons of things donated. When those donations don't pan out you can be stuck with many thousands of unplanned dollars to spend. No one ever complains about making more money than you planned. You also may have noticed that we've focused on getting our promotion and sponsorship activities in gear. I find that concert work comes in flurries: lots to do, lull, lots to do, lull, lots to do, then absolute madness on concert day. We have kicked off several lots-to-dos for promotion and it is now time to deal with the concert itself.

This book is about doing it yourself. It is based on my belief that most of the elements, when broken down properly, are not all that difficult to master. You actually can learn from reading and then doing. If you are really tight on a budget you can get by and do the job by appointing someone as your volunteer stage manager/production specialist. However, I urge you to hire a professional for this part if at all possible. If in doubt but planning to build an annual event, I recommend that you hire a professional stage manager for the first year at least in order to learn the ropes and better understand what stage management and production support is about.

I'm blessed in having a friend who is one of the best stage manager/production specialists I've ever known. She has worked with the biggest and best names in the business as well as legions of unknowns. She has worked in the finest concert halls and absolute dumps. She comes with an incredible range of contacts in unions, concert halls and the press. She knows where to find a Hammond Organ at the last minute or specialized spot lights when some are required. She knows how to read a technical contract and ask if the performer can live without a certain piece of equipment. That request alone may save a few thousand dollars. She knows what can and what cannot be done in a union hall and she can make friends with all the technicians rather than create enemies. Believe me, you want the technicians on your side when you are staging a major show. My friend, McShane Glover, agreed to sign on for this concert and gave me a very reasonable price to get us off the ground our first year out. Her fee was $4,000 when fair market would have been $6,000 to $8,000.

When we actually get to the day of the concert our deal is that I run everything in the front of the house and she runs everything behind and on the stage. She will keep the acts moving, get speakers on and off the stage, keep out gate crashers, sort the last minute problems that will arise, sort performers into dressing rooms, arrange for equipment to be delivered on time, insure that all schedules are followed and present a smooth, seamless show that appears totally relaxed to the audience. At the end of the day

she will be totally exhausted. If you choose not to hire a professional you must get a volunteer to take charge of this piece. You cannot
do it yourself. Your job is in the front of the house, overseeing the
reception, calming frazzled nerves of worried board members, making sure the governor is seated in the correct place, making sure the
green room reception is smooth and pleasant. When everyone else
gets edgy or worried, YOU must be the calm in the midst of the
storm. If you start running around in a panic then everyone else will
follow suit. The stage and backstage require full-time attention as
well. You cannot be in two places at once. You must have a stage
manager.

After reviewing the contracts for stage needs and technical
specifications, McShane immediately starts working on two time-
lines, one for the day of the concert and a second for the events leading up to the day of the concert. She will immediately get in touch
with the shop steward at the Meyerhoff and start sorting out what
we will and will not need in terms of union manpower and equipment in order to stage this concert. She will design backstage passes and special reception passes so that only people who belong
backstage will be backstage. She's tough, she even makes *me* wear
my pass. She will arrange parking permits and coordinate the loading times for equipment and musicians that are scheduled to arrive
the day before and day of the concert. We have a loading bay behind
the stage that allows for two trucks to unload at one time, we cannot have several trucks arriving at the same time and we cannot
have folks parking in the ramp, thereby blocking trucks.

We've worked together a number of times and usually sit
down and bounce ideas off of each other as we fill in our concert
schedule. The concert will start at 8 P.M., which is typical for our
area, and McShane will start us on time. You can take that to the
bank. Nothing says amateur like starting your show late. We decided that the pre-concert reception will start at 6:30 and we will shut
the bars down and move our VIPs into the theatre about 7:45. The
lobby will be open for our VIP guests to get into the reception and
the lobby proper will be open to the general public starting at 7 P.M.
McShane and I believe that less is more, so we try to keep our
announcements and introductions to a minimum. We want people
to know that this concert is about more than just Ray Charles. We
want to present The Maryland School for the Blind in a very positive light but we don't want to overpower the evening. The balance

is a delicate one so McShane and I come up with the following schedule.

TENTATIVE SCHEDULE - JUNE 20TH AT MEYERHOFF WITH RAY CHARLES

1:00 pm	Setup - 8 hands
3:00 pm	Delivery - Hammond organ, Leslie speaker cabinet & bench
4:00 pm ???	Ray Charles arrives (one tour bus)
4:30 pm	Sound check - Deanna
4:30 pm???	Presentation: Chaputier Wines to Mr. Charles (to date, no okay for same)
5:00 pm	Sound check - Ray Charles
6:00 pm	Dinner - 15? people (Deanna - 5; Local #19 - 8; MSB - 2+?)
6:30 pm	VIP reception in the lobby
7:00 pm	Doors open
7:45 pm	VIPs move into theatre

SHOW

8:00 pm	Welcome - Mary Beth Marsden, ABC (voice-over intro)
8:05 pm	Deanna Bogart
8:35 pm	Intermission - reset stage for Ray Charles
8:55 pm	Mary Beth Marsden; Jim Hollan; Lou Tutt, Howard Greenberg
9:05 pm	Ray Charles - Number with children???
10:20 pm	Finish show; start load - out
10:30 pm	Green Room reception backstage (10-15 minutes) - ? people

Notes
1 This is only a preliminary schedule; please call with corrections, especially in areas marked with ?s.

We have more detail for each moment in this show so that even the introductions and acknowledgments will be scripted in large print before show time so that they can be easily read from the podium. You will notice that the schedule starts at 1 P.M. but the fact is McShane and I will likely arrive about 10 A.M. that morning. We will go into more detail about the day of the event in the next chapter so let's concentrate on the show portion of this schedule.

At 8 P.M. sharp the house lights will go down and a voice from the dark will announce something like "Ladies and Gentlemen, The Meyeyerhoff Symphony Hall is pleased to introduce your mistress of ceremonies for this evening, the news anchor for ABC-TV2, Mary Beth Marsden." As a reminder, you need someone with an announcer-like voice to make this announcement. Mary Beth will welcome everyone, acknowledge some of the celebrities in the audience, especially the governor and the president of the school, point out why this is a special night, then introduce the first act. It all will take less than five minutes.

At 8:05 Deanna Bogart will explode onto the stage with her act for the next 30 minutes. The intermission allows time for folks to go to the lobby bars, the rest rooms or just stretch their legs as the stage is reset for Ray Charles and his band. The intermission is 20 minutes long, the house lights go down and the invisible voice intones "Ladies and Gentlemen, once again, your mistress of ceremonies, Mary Beth Marsden." This time Mary Beth will lead a short presentation program that brings our major sponsor on stage to receive thanks from our president and a ceremonial check will be presented. I've attached the script for these announcements in the next chapter. The entire process takes less than ten minutes. A special moment is observed, our major sponsors are thanked and our audience is not overburdened with long winded speeches. At 9:05 Ray Charles takes charge of the stage and keeps our crowd rocking until 10:20. We can dwell on that for a few minutes before we get back to the timeline and make sure that we are ready at the same time Ray is.

With dates and times in hand we can move into more and more detail at every level. Let's use our budget in Chapter 4 as a guidepost.

The Meyerhoff rental rate stayed the same as did the fees to rent the lobby reception area. The rates to rent major equipment like the piano, house sound, and house lights also remain the same as do the rates for box office services and house personnel. Because we are using house personnel the cost of security drops $50 and management decides not to charge us for the Green Room since we are using so many other services — that is an additional $600 savings. No fees have gone up so we are $650 under budget. The ticket is a standard format that lists every seat and price along with a stub for accurate record keeping. We get to add three lines of information to the ticket when we order them approximately 12 weeks before the show.

We had a difficult time locating the correct kind of Hammond Organ and it cost just under $500 to have it delivered and tuned, and to have a technician stand by and take it away at the

```
┌──────────────────────────────────────────────────────────────────────────┐
│                    JOSEPH MEYERHOFF SYMPHONY HALL                          │
│   ORCHESTRA          Baltimore Symphony Orchestra           ORCHESTRA      │
│                     David Zinman • Music Director                          │
│   CENTER             Sun Jun. 28, 1998  7:00 PM             CENTER         │
│  LOCATION                                                  LOCATION        │
│    H    109          The Smothers Brothers        H    109                 │
│  ROW   SEAT                    and                 ROW   SEAT              │
│  EVENT  970628 R         The Kingston Trio         EVENT  970628 R         │
│  PATRON #                                          DATE   06/28/98         │
│         214557                                     TIME      7:00 PM       │
│                                                                            │
│  PRICE                                             PRICE                    │
├──────────────────────────────────────────────────────────────────────────┤
│ Latecomers will be seated at suitable intervals. Programs and artists      │
│ subject to change. No refunds. No smoking.                                 │
└──────────────────────────────────────────────────────────────────────────┘
```

end of the concert. I'm thinking of going into the instrument rental business with rates like this! Thanks to McShane and the shop steward we have worked out a new estimate of union labor that is about $1,000 less than our original estimate. Our updated estimate of production costs is $1,650 less than our first estimate: we are on the right track.

Our major sponsor gets their name on top of the 40 foot x 4 foot banner that hangs above the stage. Gold and major media sponsors get a less prominent display on the same banner. The banner will read:

SMITH, SOMERVILLE & CASE
present
Ray Charles
in a concert to benefit
THE MARYLAND SCHOOL FOR THE BLIND

We call a few sign companies and they quote $800 to $1,200 for the banner and $125 to $225 for the ceremonial presentation check. We negotiate with one company to deliver both for a total of $800 which was our budgeted amount. It is not required that we feed the crews but it is an excellent policy. We will have our own volunteers on hand all day long and it is just as easy to have food brought in for an additional eight or 10 people. It additionally goes a long way toward building good will. More about that later.

We have come up with an opening act for $400 less than estimated, our photographer has donated her time saving us an additional $500 and, thanks to a donation of wine, our VIP reception is likely to be at least $1,500 less than estimated. The official printed program is moving forward as outlined in Chapter 8. The printer we are working with normally produces our annual report and several other printed products for the school. The first bid for our program, flyers and a color poster came in a little over $7,500 for printing, way over our $5,000 budget. The printer agreed to cut the bill by $3,500 and we agreed to list them as a Silver Sponsor and give them four VIP tickets. That keeps us running under budget and it gets more of our sponsors actively involved. I want my sponsors at the VIP reception because I think they will have such a good time that they will be delighted to return the following year. They are even likely to move up in their sponsorship level.

We have also divided up the seating charts for our VIP guests so that they have the best seating. We make a point of scattering the celebrity guest seating throughout the VIP group and we try, when aware of any problems, to separate folks who might not get along. Our caterers are working on a special menu for us and we are working to get the best bang for our buck at every level. We will focus on making this special event "special" and we will concentrate on getting as much publicity as possible. We started well with our sponsorship dollars but we must have a successful box office if we hope to realize our goals.

Chapter II
The Day Of the Concert

I'm a "Nervous Nelly," the type who arrives at the airport at least three hours before my flight. My wife, the saint, just lets me go crazy, even when I'm packed for a trip two days before we leave. Having said that, you will better understand why I arrive at the Meyerhoff about nine or 10 in the morning. I don't need to be there that early but I'd just as soon worry on site as worry at home. If home, I might convince myself that my car will be stuck in traffic for 10 hours on the way to Baltimore and I'd miss the concert. Everyone is glad when I just go to the concert hall and work out my anxiety. Remember, I'm the one who is supposed to be calm as we approach show time. The fact is that I usually am and I think that leaving plenty of time for things to work themselves out contributes to that calm.

I usually bring a gym bag filled with stuff that I might and often do need. I bring a hammer, screwdrivers and pliers, various size nails, scotch tape, push pins, string, a needle and thread, a staple gun, magic markers, pens, blank paper, a flashlight and other odd bits based on my anxiety level. I always get a dressing room for myself to act as a collecting place, center of operations and place to change before the show. I dress in jeans and workshirt for the day; consequently, I bring my clothes for the evening, toiletries and an extra towel for a pre-show shower. Prior to the concert we have assigned dressing rooms. Just behind and off centerstage are two major and one minor dressing room. The major goes to Ray Charles, one minor to Deanna Bogart, our opening act, and one for Mary

Beth Marsden, our mistress of ceremonies. Downstairs we have various soloist and group dressing rooms. I get a soloist room for myself with private bath and shower, and we assign two group dressing rooms to the Ray Charles band and another for Deanna Bogart's band. One of the lovely things about a big symphony hall is the abundance of dressing rooms and lounges.

We've printed up signs on our computer and I dig these out and go around taping signs to doors. Nothing is so professional or satisfying as seeing your name on the dressing room door. I also check to make sure the rooms are fresh and clean. Towels will be delivered later in the day, a few hours before show time. I also leave a few copies of the printed program and an updated copy of the timeline for this evening's show.

McShane worries almost as much as I do and she arrives shortly after me with a few dozen donuts and coffee pots. Everyone is always glad to see her for some reason. McShane and I review notes for the ten-thousandth time. Ticket sales have been slower than we anticipated but we were featured as a "Baltimore's Best Bet" in yesterday's *Baltimore Sun* and our TV sponsor has been giving us a lot of on-air support the last two days; consequently, our sales have picked up quite a bit within the last 48 hours. We review the latest report from the box office and we still have about 800 seats available — disappointing, but there's nothing we can do to change that at this time. We focus, instead, on those things we can do something about.

The stage crews start wandering in shortly after noon and countless cables, electrical cords, lights, wires, microphones, risers and other tools of the trade start to appear. Various lights are moved and tested, huge panels come to life as the technical directions on paper get transcribed to the stage. The Grand Piano is rolled into place, tuned and tested. The Hammond Organ arrives and is likewise tuned and arranged. A local deli delivers trays of cold cuts to the lounge along with cookies. Sodas are set up next to the coffee pots for the crews and volunteers. Caterers show up from Spike and Charlie's to dress the tables and bars in the lobby reception area. They go to work with pins and cloth, then arrange beautiful slabs of rock, slate and marble on top of that; these will be the showplace display pieces for the food that will arrive later in the day.

Ray Charles has sent his sound and light specifications. When everything is tested and tuned, the set up is moved and the crews go to work on the set up for Deanna Bogart, the opening act. Deanna arrives at four with her band and they go on stage to test the set up of equipment at 4:30. The process takes over an hour. Stage crews lift the show banner into place above the stage as maintenance crews polish everything that can be polished. The hall manager checks in on us a few times to make sure that everything is moving along well. Ray Charles is supposed to arrive at 4:15 and we have scheduled a special presentation of an autographed three-liter bottle of wine from Chapoutier in France. By five there is still no Ray Charles. More troubling is the fact that the union is scheduled to load Ray and his band in starting at 4:30. They are scheduled for dinner at 6 P.M.

I've checked in with the caterers as the food arrives, verified that the programs are ready to be handed out by the house staff, checked again with the box office — we've sold another 100 tickets — and then moved downstairs to my dressing room for a shower and to change into my tuxedo. McShane has control of the stage, Ray still hasn't arrived by six and I need to go to the front of the house to get my VIP volunteers ready for our reception. Ray and his band arrive at 6:30 just as my reception starts. The knot in my stomach eases up a bit with this news but my job is with the reception. I find out later from McShane that the union guys just interrupt their dinner and load Ray and his band in. This is very generous of them. As this is a "Union House" they could simply wait until dinner was over and then load the band in, making the show run late and gaining overtime for themselves. That was their legal right but these guys tell us not to worry and go out of their way to make sure our event goes off smoothly. Remember what I said about treating people right and they will do the same for you?

We move our VIP crowd into the theatre and I go behind stage to deliver the final payment for the show to Ray's representative. This is a common practice in our business and you shouldn't be offended when asked to pay by certified check before the performance. The music business has a long history of non payment and musicians have learned the hard way over the years to get paid first. House lights go down, the voice over announces our mistress of ceremonies as Mary Beth Marsden walks on stage. The show has begun.

Having a local news anchor as a host for the evening works at many different levels. They are not only famous locally, they are also familiar, someone the audience feels they know and that was clear from the moment Mary Beth walked on stage. She welcomed everyone on behalf of the school, acknowledged a few of the celebrities in the audience (we told her where they were located since you can't see a damn thing from the stage with spotlights in your face), then she moved quickly to the introductions for our opening act by asking the audience to welcome Deanna Bogart. As the applause started, Mary Beth left and Deanna took charge of the stage for a terrific, up tempo, rock and roll, boogie woogie opening act that had the audience up on their feet. She was unknown to most in the crowd and a real surprise when they realized how good she was. At 8:39 she took her final bow and the audience got up to shake out their limbs, go to the rest room or hit one of the bars around the theater for a glass of wine or a soda.

At 8:57 the house lights went down again and at 8:59 the invisible voice over asked the audience to once again welcome Mary Beth Marsden. This time we will actually get a chance to make our presentations and have our brief moment in the sun. We script all of it well ahead of time and then we time the process. We do not want to run over 10 minutes for all of this business

---

Introduction 2
8:55 p.m.
(approximate)

Off Stage Voice: Ladies and Gentlemen, once again, your mistress of ceremonies, Mary Beth Marsden.
Mary Beth — Thank you . . . Thank you
Welcome Back.
Now before we move to our feature attraction this evening
We need to acknowledge a few very special people.
As you know an event like this is not possible without many planners, many workers and many supporters.
But someone has to be in charge.

Someone has to gather all the elements together in order for us all to be here.

In this case that someone is the Director of Development at The Maryland School for the Blind — the man who put this concert all together — Mr. Jim Hollan.

Jim Enters

Jim: Thank you Mary Beth, thank you all.
Since we are thanking people I think this is a perfect time to thank our gracious Mistress of Ceremonies, the remarkable Mary Beth Marsden, for adding such a touch of class to this evening's event.
(Applause)

Mary Beth: Thank you Jim, thank you all.

Jim: Mary Beth is quite correct, an event like this requires the support and cooperation of many people and we thank each and every one of you from the bottom of our hearts, in particular we thank our silver and gold sponsors whose generosity seems to have no bounds. Please look at the names in your program and recognize them for the kind of corporate citizens they are. We thank them all.

For a special acknowledgement I'd like to present the president of The Maryland School for the Blind, Louis M. Tutt.

Lou Tutt comes on stage.

Lou Tutt: Thank you Jim, thank you Mary Beth, and let me add my thanks to all of you for being here tonight but we must single out one name in particular.
The name on top of that banner — (turn and point)
the major sponsor for this evening.
Smith, Somerville and Case.

The ties between this prestigious law firm and The Maryland School for the Blind are long and deep, it is not a new relationship as the firm has been represented on our Board of Directors since the firm was founded.

When Jim Hollan proposed this concert as a friend and a fund raiser it was quite a challenge to our board as an event of this size requires quite a large financial committment. Within moments of the proposal, Mike Kelly, a partner in the law firm of Smith, Somerville and Case and a member of our Board of Directors for years stood up and announced that his firm would be glad to act as the major sponsor for this event. You can't imagine how surprised and how delighted we were.

For a special presentation I would like to introduce Mike Kelly from our Board of Directors and the Chairman of the Executive Committee at Smith, Somerville and Case, Mr. Howard Goldberg.

Howard and Mike enter: (Maybe Mike carries check and Howard speaks at podium — keep check turned in so amount can't be seen.)

Howard: Thank you Lou and thank you one and all.

I can't tell you how delighted I am to be here in such prestigious company. It is an honor for our firm to be associated with The Maryland School for the Blind. An honor to work with such a caring and dedicated organization, an organization faithfully serving the children of Maryland for over 144 years.

Lou — I am simply the spokesman for every member of our firm and we thank you for what you and your staff do each and every day. We are grateful for this opportunity to do our small part.

This is the first event of its type for the school and I'm pleased to be the guy who announces the good news.

Lou and Jim — Mike Kelly, a partner in our firm and member of your Board of Directors, is holding a check that represents the total amount raised by this year's concert.

Mary Beth, perhaps you will do the honors. (Howard hands paper with number to Mary Beth and steps to Mike's side as they turn and present the check to Lou and Jim — Mary Beth will read the amount — we will smile, Mike and I hold check as Lou and Howard shake hands — we four walk off stage — Jim will carry check. There will be a quick practice behind the curtain before we go on stage so we know which side to exit and enter.)

Mary Beth: Announces the amount when the check is presented (will be on paper at podium)

(Applause as amount announced, we shake hands and exit.)

Isn't that wonderful? I must say this is a great way to raise money. . . . A lot more enjoyable than those late night phone calls. . . . . .

Now let's get down to the main event for this evening.

He is a national treasure and an international phenomenon.
He is the American Dream — raised in poverty, triumphing over tragedy, overcoming adversity . . .
He has a Star on Hollywood Boulevard's Walk of Fame.
He is in the Rock and Roll Hall of Fame.
He is in the Jazz Hall of Fame.
He is in the Rhythm & Blues Hall of Fame.
He has 12 Grammys.
He has innumerable Gold records.
He has countless awards, including the National Medal of Arts presented by President Bill Clinton.

I could talk about him all night.
Like most of you I'm sure, his songs are often sign posts in my life.
Rather than talk about him
I'm delighted to introduce one of the greatest musicians of our time.
Ladies and Gentlemen,
The amazing Ray Charles.

With the final introduction, The Ray Charles Band starts a four or five minute musical introduction that builds and builds until Ray himself walks onto the stage with the largest smile known to man and the audience is up on their feet. The show is spectacular as Ray and the band move from hit to hit, the final segments featuring the Rayletts. I even have enough time to go to the back of the concert hall and look down at the end result of my hard work. It is a very exciting moment for me, but the night isn't over yet. I still have a major donor event to come at the meet and greet so I watch for a few minutes then move on to check the setup in the Green Room.

The concert ends, Ray goes to his dressing room as our special guests move to the Green Room area behind stage. We have security at the door, which is absolutely mandatory, since quite a few people try to get back stage to see Ray. The caterer has prepared a wonderful selection of desserts served with coffee or tea. The early arrivals mix and chat, delighted with the show. In addition to my own photographer we have arranged for the social columnist from *The Sun* to cover the meet and greet and she has sent along an additional photographer. Nothing makes your major sponsors happier than seeing their photos in the social pages in the days following your event. It's also a nice reminder for those who declined your offer to sponsor; perhaps they will rethink that decision next year.

Ray finally arrives and we are able to have a presentation made by the nice people who sponsored our wine and then we get all the group photos that we need. Ray is a little tired, a touch grumpy and ready to leave quickly, when he realizes that a few of our blind students are also in the group. Suddenly he has all the time in the world to chat and smile and encourage these kids. It is a lovely visit and Ray is off with a final good-bye.

The band is packing up and loading the buses for a drive tonight and set up for tomorrow's concert at Wolftrap in Virginia. The stage crew is breaking down the stage and the hall staff is already sorting out the theater and lobby as my guests mix and mingle for several additional minutes after Ray leaves. A few reception stragglers need a little nudging to get them on their way and we close the doors. I go down to the dressing room and pack up my bags of stuff to take home. I then take a final backstage tour to make sure everything is under control. McShane reports that all is well and we congratulate each other on a job well done. It is our custom not to talk for a few days as we are too close to the event and we have been talking far too much in the final days approaching the concert.

I realize that I'm starving. The food has been spectacular but I've been so busy that I've never had time to stop for a moment and eat anything. I've been too busy worrying and supervising. John Peltz, the catering manager from Spike and Charlie's comes up and hands me two small bags of food, a selection from the reception and the meet and greet. He smiles and points out that this is usually the case for the person in charge and they always prepare a little take-home bag. I am immeasurably grateful as I collect my belongings and head home where I will sleep for 12 hours. The entire process is totally exhausting and extraordinarily satisfying.

Chapter 12
The Small Concert

It would be very convenient indeed, if I could say that a small concert is the same as a large concert only smaller; however, that is not the case. In many ways the small concert is actually more difficult to pull off. Once things get large, when well known performers and concert halls are involved, most people are a bit intimidated and they back off a bit. They may worry you to death with questions, but they generally don't interfere because they realize they don't really know what they are doing and they don't want to appear stupid. Sadly, no such restrictions exist when it comes to a smaller, local concert. In fact, it seems that the amount of unsolicited advice and annoyingly time consuming interference received is inversely proportional to the size of the venue.

Everyone is an expert when it comes to local productions. Members of the board who cannot find time to work on the event, nonetheless, will call to give you meaningful tidbits of advice or, even more annoying, call to challenge decisions made by you and your committee. Local venues will often act as if they are The Metropolitan Opera and you are an illiterate baboon. Local arts groups will flex their muscle as they believe they "own" the arts locally and you are something of an interloper. I can certainly think of some exceptions, but experience has taught me that smaller concerts are usually more trouble than larger ones. Odd isn't it?

In order to not embarrass the guilty or get myself involved in a lawsuit, let me summarize some problems I've encountered over the years with smaller events. The people referred to are all clearly figments of my imagination and bear no resemblance whatsoever to real idiots that I have known.

- An organization held an annual event that had been waning over the last few years. The executive director decided that something new on that same date was needed and moved to hold a concert as a new fund raising event. A few months into the planning he decided that it was a mistake to abandon the original event and he simply reinstated it. He saw no conflict since the reinstated event was held in the day and the concert would be in the evening. Staff was suddenly over stretched for planning, board members were divided in their loyalties to one event or the other and there was now limited focus on both events. The daytime event took so much energy that workers were too tired to come to the evening event and very few volunteers were available for afternoon concert setup since so many were involved with the other daytime event. In fact the executive director failed to show up as he was too tired. Both events were a disaster. I was young and stupid and swore this would never happen to me again.

- Instead of asking for the hall rental rates at a local center for the arts, I made the mistake of telling them what I was planning to do. The hall took it upon themselves to adjust their rates upwards according to the type of act I was going to have and they demanded a copy of our contract with the performer. Unbeknownst to me, they had tried and failed to book this same performer the year before. When I explained that was not an appropriate request, they pointed out that "they" were the experts and their behavior was typical among "professionals." Our show would have been one of the most prestigious ever hosted at this venue and it would have provided a handsome profit for a grossly underutilized facility. We bit the bullet and said no. We moved to another venue outside our home town which turned out to be great and we put on a successful event, but we were less satisfied than we should have been. We wanted to make this a "home town" event but a greedy and unprofessional venue forced us to move elsewhere. As a footnote, the director of that venue was gone a year later.

- We had a local venue owned by a non profit send us a contract for the facility rental. We added a number of provisions that had been discussed on the phone but were not in the contract. These referred to use of space for a pre-concert VIP reception, selling beverages in a hallway and use of a special gallery for an after-concert meet and greet. The venue initialed the changes and signed the contract. On concert day our setup crews were informed that the VIP and meet and greet spaces were not available as the venue had rented them out to someone else. After several hours of delay the hall manager was still unwilling to admit my teams to these spaces for setup as he thought the contract was not valid since we had "...added a bunch of changes that were not normal." Even a threat of a lawsuit proved useless as he stated "you can't sue a non profit" (*He was wrong about that*). Fortunately we were able to track down the chairman of the board of directors of this non profit and with a lot of arm twisting from influential members of our board we got him to instruct the hall manager to honor the signed contract. Hours were wasted, anxiety levels were needlessly elevated and a bad taste was left in the mouth of many volunteer participants. In case you missed it, the point here is to get it in writing. In this case I don't think the hall manager was trying to be coy, I just think he wasn't very smart. We would have been dead in the water if we had not written in our verbal agreements and made sure he signed them.

When you host a smaller concert the same basic policies and principles we've discussed so far apply for most of what you do. All the same elements come into play with a shift in scale and you must shift your strategy accordingly. You pay for fame. Big names, big dollars. As you move down the scale you get performers who are less well known, often performers who need some explaining. By that I mean you generally give the name of the performer, encounter a blank stare, then add an explanation like "You know, he had that hit record in the 60s called ...." or "She was the daughter on that TV series in the 70s."

You can use the same sources as listed in Chapter 3 in your search for a main act. As you move a bit further down the list of performers you are also likely to move a bit further down on the list of agents. Smaller agencies are the same as large ones, some are great and some are lousy. Many specialize in certain kinds of acts, oldies, jazz, folk, rock, etc. Some of these agencies package acts into a show that might give you the best bang for your bucks. An act from the 70s that had three hit records might not be a big draw on their own, but an agency might package three or four such acts into a show with a small backup band. Suddenly you have a "Fabulous Stars of the 70s" show rather than one lesser known act.

Smaller agencies are usually a lot more flexible than big ones and they require a bit more caution, however, you often have a lot more negotiating room. Big agencies don't rely on the likes of us for their big dollars. We are small change. We might book one or two acts a year whereas they prefer dealing with people who book 40 or 50 or more acts a year. The big agencies use us to fill in the blank spots between performances whereas the smaller agencies often rely on a convoluted network of people just like us to paste together a night here and a weekend there for their acts. The budgets are smaller and the expectations are smaller. I've had acts quoted at $40,000 for the entire show and listened over the course of several months as the same act has dropped to $35,000, then $30,000, then $25,000, then a request to "make me an offer." A request for $15,000 plus first-class airfare for the performer and three backup musicians was eventually negotiated down to $7,000 flat plus three hotel rooms for one night. On another occasion we said no to a $20,000 act. Two weeks later we had a call back from the agency asking if the date was still open. We said it was, a Friday night. We fell between a booking the weekend before south of us and a Saturday just to the north; rather than return home to California it made more sense to take a discount for a venue in-route and we agreed on $8,000 for the night. I have also worked out percentages with smaller agencies. For example we had a hall that sat 800 and we settled on a base rate of $5,000 for the act. If we sold more than 500 seats the act would receive an additional $1,000 and if we sold more than 700 seats the act received another $1,000. It was a way for us to hedge against the possibility of not selling out for a smaller concert. Many variations of these deals are out there. You will sometimes run into rates for performers that are completely a percentage of the gate; however, you must balance these percentages against the goals and objectives of your organization. What I'm getting at is that percentage deals often leave the non profit sponsor with a miniscule profit. Some are legitimate but it is an area that requires careful examination.

Your press coverage will likely not include TV and the range of coverage in print will also be less since less well known acts are less newsworthy. Don't take it personally when you get less coverage than big event non profits in nearby cities. There is a proportionality to things and small concerts operate at a smaller scale; nevertheless, you must maximize what you have. Get those press releases out to as many possible outlets as you can think of and have the same kind of press release plan as we discussed in Chapter 6. Don't just assume that local papers will give you coverage simply because you are you. Get out there and sell your event so that you can maximize coverage.

Small towns generally don't have television stations but they usually have radio stations, which should become a focus for your event. Get them involved in sponsoring your concert. Generate a radio contest with seats as prizes. Arrange for a phone-in interview several weeks before the concert with your main act. Get your station to feature the hits of your performer. Give them something to work with and get them talking about your event. Get them to make it *their* event.

The scale of sponsorship also moves down a bit but the principle of a main sponsor and secondary sponsors should still hold. Know that many local branches of state or national banks and utilities have a local cap on donations that are given at the discretion of the local manager. The prices you can charge for your tickets are likely to be less than your big-time counterparts, which means that you are looking at less income from all the key sources. So why do a small concert?

Actually there are a lot of good reasons to start small. Perhaps the most basic is that you can only afford to finance a small concert. I've made it clear that small concerts can grow into big concerts as long as you keep your eyes on the prize and plan for growth over several years. Yes, your potential income is a lot less than the big concert but the expenses are often a lot less also. Smaller venues are usually a lot less expensive to rent; some actually donate the space. The programs need not be very elaborate and the posters can be smaller and one color. The VIP reception should still be special and the meet and greet might actually become part of the reception itself but the scale need not be as grand as the one for your major concert. Everything changes proportionally, but all the elements still come into play. Instead of a union crew, you are likely to be dealing with a local sound/lights guy who does this on a part-time basis. The house staff is likely to be a crew of volunteers you've recruited and you might even have a local printer make up and donate the tickets. You might take in a lot less, spend a lot less, make a reasonable profit to reinvest in the following year while gaining experience in production. It's like getting paid to go to concert production school. Two or three years down the road you have hands-on experience, a knowledgeable staff of volunteers, a track record of success and enough money in the bank to step up to the big event.

On occasion a small concert can be far more successful that a large concert. About 15 years ago a local venue with limited funds came up with the idea of staging a Gospel Competition. They put up a $1,000 prize, invested a few thousand more in judges fees, posters, programs, mailings and some technical costs for first-rate sound and sound technicians. The venue was donated and the concert was a sellout with many small sponsors lining up for this colorful event. For an investment of less than $5,000 they produced a net profit of almost $25,000 and quickly established an annual statewide event that grew into a week-long competition ending in the final concert. Everyone wanted to be the "best" in the state.

Starting small requires patience but it can work. If in doubt remember the example of The Hard Travelers in Chapter 1 or focus on the success of P. Michael Meyerstein in Chapter 14. Michael has 1,500 seats at Temple Beth Tfiloh and he stages an annual concert that nets $300,000 after expenses! And it's still growing! As you will see, Michael has given new definition to the meaning of success in small places.

Chapter 13
Very Large Concerts

As dumb as it sounds, moving up to a *really* big concert from a successful big concert is terrifying and risky. It also requires careful consideration. A concert in, let's say, the 2,500 seat range will develop a life of its own. You will get a core of VIPs that return year after year so that your VIP reception and the ticket sales associated with it grow each year. Certain corporate sponsors will make your concert a company event and they will take responsibility for a certain number of tickets. The fact is that you can eventually go into a concert knowing that you will have 1,000 or 1,500 tickets sold before you've even settled on a performer. The concert event itself will have a following. It sure takes the pressure off when you build on your strengths and only worry about selling another 1,000 tickets or so. A successful event becomes easier to manage each year as you master the fine points. Moving up to a bigger venue is a whole new ballgame.

You will rarely run into a series of venue steps that go from 2,500 seats to 4,500 seats to 7,000 seats and so on. In our area the step up from the few venues in the 2,500 to 3,000 range is to the 13,000 range. Nothing like the prospect of selling three or four times as many seats to the same geographic population! Even more intimidating is the last step which moves you up to the 50,000+ stadium level. The same principles apply but the range of skills needed for success also moves up the scale. Costs increase significantly, services at every level will require professionals and there will be very little room for amateur mistakes.

I must admit to having mixed feelings about very large concerts. I find them intimidating yet I'm drawn to their possibilities. Big venues allow you to call on the biggest names in the business. Performers at this level are often associated with large international tour sponsors, allowing you the option to tie in with some of these sponsorships and it is easier to call on your local sponsors when you are offering association with a real superstar. However, I've found that you can negotiate very little with superacts. They generally have a routine and they cannot afford to deviate much. Some are not at all interested in meet and greets and they can now afford to say "No." At this level you often see a number of big trucks and buses show up early in the day to off load a crew of "roadies" who set the equipment and the stage. Shortly before the show, the feature performer will show up, perform and leave. The roadies spend several hours breaking down, loading up and moving on to the next spot.

Once again, agents are more interested in the big bookers, the big promoters, who might book 40 or 50 acts or 40 or 50 engagements for the same act rather than once a year bookers like us. Even for the very big dollar acts, I've found that we are generally not all that well treated by agencies. We are the fill-in after the big dates and big promoters are satisfied. It is what it is, nothing personal.

At a venue for 13,000 people you might be looking at projected ticket sales in the $350,000 range, VIP sales approaching $100,000 and an additional $250,000 in sponsor dollars. Seven-hundred thousand dollars flowing into your coffers to offset what? Even with all your advertising and promotion donated, you will likely spend $150,000 to $250,000 for your main act and your production costs can run another $100,000 to $250,000. If you take in $700,000 and your costs are $250,000, well you suddenly become the best thing since sliced bread, earning a $450,000 profit for your organization. If ticket sales and sponsorships are a bit softer than anticipated and you only take in $550,000 and your costs are at the higher end, let's say $450,000, then you've done okay for your first year out. You made a $100,000 profit for your cause and you've gained a lot of new friends along with positive publicity. Your costs are pretty high relative to your net profit, but you are on the right track. You should get much better in the future.

We can't stop here however. It could be that we overestimated the draw for our main act and our ticket sales were only $110,000, VIP sales amounted to $40,000 and sponsorships were only

$150,000. If expenses are once again $450,000, we have just worked our buns off and gone in the hole for $150,000. Now you are a pariah; moreover, this year's sponsors are not likely to be next year's sponsors. They came to a big event with lots of empty seats. It's the classic "What if you threw a party and nobody came?" If the show failed they will not blame the performer — after all, the performer is famous. They will blame you. They will probably be right.

Even though I've been involved with many concerts over the years, I enter the gates of very large venues with trepidation. At this level of performance, the performer and the venue are really not much of a problem. Both are so professional that they are almost self contained. Venues of this size are staffed by specialists who have seen it all. It may be a big deal for you, but the venue hosted a hockey game for 13,000 last night, your event tonight and maybe the touring Military Bands of Great Britain tomorrow night. They will do their jobs and do them well, meaning you worry less about what goes on behind the scenes at venues this size. You put the extra time and energy into worrying about the promotional end of your show. I must say that as the size of the concert grows the fine line between regular promoter and non-profit fund raiser gets blurred for me. Perhaps the key difference at this point is the non profit's ability to call on charitable sponsors for support. In all of our profit and loss projections, contributions, in the form of sponsorships, have been the key to our success. With advance apologies to those of you who already know this, I must take a few minutes to talk about contributions and responsible fund raising.

Successful fund raising is a function of the bottom line, not the top line — not the total dollars raised but the total profit after all expenses are paid. All fund raisers have a responsibility to keep their cost of fund raising at a reasonable level. We are all well aware of the bums and rip-off artists in our field who raise vast sums in the name of charity only to pocket 95% of the dollars generated, passing along a pittance to the organization. Every fund-raising professional has legitimate expenses. From printing costs and postage to the salaries of the people who send out the letters and count the dollars coming in, there are very legitimate costs associated with fund raising. The attorneys general in most states have established suggested guidelines as have a number of national fund-raising organizations. Rules of thumb are just that, approximations that are not set in stone but operate as reasonable guidelines. The range floats a bit, but it is safe to say that most organizations look to have their cost of fund raising be no more than 25% of the total dollars raised. Many organizations, especially very large ones, keep their cost of fund raising at 12% to 15%. It is not uncommon for start up fund-raising efforts to run above 50% for the first year or two out as they establish themselves. Now these costs reflect *all* fund-raising efforts from the Annual Appeal through dollars generated by grant writing. It is a mix, and not every element in that mix will cost the same; moreover, fund raising is an art not a science. You will generally make the correct decision but you will occasionally make mistakes, that's the nature of our business.

Recognizing that our overall fund raising efforts for the year should keep costs down in the 15% to 30% range we can get a sense as to what our concert net profit should be. I've found that some folks confuse net profit and income. Income is the total of all dollars coming into your event. Add up all the ticket sales, sponsor dollars and any other contributions of money (not services or gifts in kind) and you have the total income. When you subtract all the costs involved with staging your event you are left with the net profit. Got it? Net profit = income minus expenses.

A start-up concert is the hardest one to get going and it is the most costly, especially when you are setting up an *annual* event. Unlike a one time happening where you are in and out to maximize your profit, an annual event requires an investment in the future as well as the present. You are planning to make more money next year and the year after; consequently, you are spending dollars now for income now and in the future. In other words, the cost of your first-year event is likely to be high. Over the first few years of your event the cost (in terms of a percentage) should go down as the net profit goes up. This is an *investment* in the future and it is not uncommon to see costs run as high as 70% to 90% the first year out. Yes, that is a very high cost, but it is the first year out and you should be able to improve quickly from that point. The follow up to a successful first concert will generally see total income go up, total costs (in terms of percentage) go down and net profit go up. A *very general* rule of thumb would post second-year costs in the 50% range and that figure should continue its downward trend over the next few years.

I've debated on more than one occasion the position that the costs of a concert are simply too high, especially the very large concert. My response is that many of the dollars raised by concerts are not normally available to the non-profit organization, they are dollars that exist in a gray area mixing contribution, promotion and entertainment dollars. In other words, you might approach a corporation for a pure contribution for your cause and receive nothing because the corporation already has a full slate of causes they support or you might receive a token sponsorship in the $500 to $1,000 range. When you approach the same corporation with the opportunity to sponsor a concert they may see an opportunity to add promotional dollars. They might see their association with the concert as an advertising opportunity and they may add advertising dollars. If the corporation is excited about the performer they might also add dollars based on the entertainment value of the act. In other words, they want to meet Ray Charles or Tommy Smothers. You are now looking at a $5,000 contribution you would not have seen otherwise. You may pay a higher percentage to raise those dollars but they are new dollars to your organization and the net profit to your organization is higher than your original solicitation. Most importantly, you now have the opportunity to grow a new contributor into a more involved contributor.

The benefit of a very large concert is that it can generate very big dollars. Some of the best known events in the country have a net profit in excess of a million. Several acts, like Rosie O'Donnell, can raise several million in one evening. Those kinds of dollars have significant impact on an organization. It is a very risky venture, but properly managed, it can more realistically raise many hundreds of thousands of dollars while keeping the name of your organization in front of the public. Remember, the concert is a tool and it is likely not to be a tool you will need to use; however, in the right situation, it well may be the exact thing you need.

Chapter 14
Talking to the Experts

The nice thing about writing your own book is that you get to express your opinion about everything and anything. If someone out there wants to disagree, well then, they just have to go and write their own book, don't they? I'm originally from New York City, which means I pretty much know everything about everything; however, on the rare chance that someone might have another point of view, I've asked some experts in the field of concert production to share their views with you. I've explained to each that this book is designed primarily for non profit organizations considering a concert as a fund-raising event. This book does not say that non profits should or should not hold such an event, rather, it is an inside look at what is involved in staging a concert so that the organization can make a more informed decision. My bias is that I love concerts and I think that they often have a place in the mix of fund-raising tools available to organizations. I also make it perfectly clear that concerts are not for everybody. In that framework, I've asked these experts to share their thoughts on a few key elements so that my readers will have a better sense as to what the professionals think. I've saved this section for late in the book so that the reader has moved all the way through the concert planning process. They now have a pretty good idea as to how the process works and it seems the perfect time to get a little additional insight from the pros.

Kenn Roberts is the driving force behind The Hard Travelers and, more than anyone, he is the key to the extraordinarily successful concerts held to benefit Cystic Fibrosis. Starting with a collection of friends, he's held concerts over the years with a panoply of stars including Barbara Mandrell, The Oak Ridge Boys, Kenny Rogers, John Denver, Alabama and Randy Travis just to name a few. Kenn has been the first in line to help many other non-profit organizations get their events off the ground. When not playing music or skiing in Colorado, Kenn is, among other things, the chairman of The Muse Foundation. He is also a very modest man and he hates being called "an expert," but since this is my book I get to call him what I want.

Jim Hollan — Kenn, let's start with the question I imagine you are asked most often. What is the first thing that comes to mind when you are asked about the merits of using a major concert as a fund-raising event?

Kenn Roberts — As a result of knowing what we do and how we do it, and having talked to many other charities that have attempted to come into this arena, my advice, first and foremost, is that concerts are not the glamorous, "can't miss" event that everybody thinks they are. They are a business and they need to be treated that way. If not run properly the whole thing becomes an exercise in futility.

If this sounds like I'm trying to scare some people off, I hope I do. Unless you have a top notch committee with at least one key person that knows what they are doing, you're going to get burned. For that same amount of effort you might make twice as much money having a stair climb or a walk or a bachelor auction. If you know what you're doing and you have the right people in your organization, there is no question that you can make money for your charity, but it is a very sophisticated business. You will be involved with entertainers, venues, sound, lighting, transportation, publicity, housing and a whole list of other skills. You almost have to be a promoter. Now that's my advice. It may not be what you want to hear but I have a strong feeling that too many people think this is a way to make money without realizing how much hard work and planning is involved.

Jim Hollan — I must say that I agree with you. I've run into more than one charity which figures if Group A can present a concert then they must be able to do the same. I know of one executive director who ordered a staff member to put on a concert as part of her job even though no one had any experience whatsoever.

Kenn Roberts — The one premise that I hear all the time is that people feel that they have a good cause therefore entertainers are just dying to come and do a concert for them free. It just isn't correct. All of these entertainers have causes, they all do some free concerts in support of their causes, but they make their living getting paid to perform. They get thousands of requests for "free" concerts and you might actually get lucky once if you have some sort of connection to their special cause or you have an inside contact, but nine times out of 10 you must pay the going rate for their services. You will be right in the pot with all the promoters who are there every day. It's a tough game. It's exasperating. I will tell you that I'm negotiating with a major performer right now and I can't wait until we get a contract so I can get down to the easy part of the job which is going to sponsors and going to people and asking them to give me money. That part we find easy compared to putting the concert together — that's the tough part.

Jim Hollan — If a local non profit is committed to trying a concert as a fund raiser and they have the funds to start small or actually start with a larger venue right off the bat, what would your advice be on their strategy?

Kenn Roberts — Assuming that this particular charity does not have a direct link to Celine Dion or someone of that stature who will appear absolutely for free then I recommend you start small and grow. It's a learning curve. It's a business in every respect. Start small, learn the business and grow.

Jim Hollan — What are some of the major mistakes, the obvious mistakes you see repeated by groups in the start-up stage?

Kenn Roberts — It definitely falls back to my original statement. People are unaware of the costs involved, the planning involved, the many small pieces that come into play. The biggest mistake is not having a good organization of people, both volunteer and professional, working on your event. You can't have the executive director call the promoter, then have the promoter make a few calls and have a few thousand people show up at a venue for a concert.

It just doesn't work that way. You must have an organization that works well together.

Jim Hollan — I spend a lot of time in the book talking about where I make my money and I focus on the VIP reception and the meet and greet. The fact is that much of what works for me I've copied from your events. Can you talk a bit about how you use the VIP reception and meet and greet for your event? I see them as events within events.

Kenn Roberts — Well it's really pretty simple. You have some limited number of tickets that give people a reception, better seats and, more than anything, you give them the title of VIPs. I've tried for years to come up with a better title but this one seems to work. People like being called VIP and we make a sizable amount of money from that portion of ticket sales. The meet and greet on the other hand is becoming less important. Fewer big name entertainers are willing to attend. I have to tell you in all honesty, because I'm an entertainer, I understand a bit about that unwillingness. Before the concert you are focused on your performance and really don't want to mix with people and after the concert you just want to unwind and be relaxed. It's very difficult to have a lot of people clawing over you when you are emotionally beat.

Jim Hollan — What do you see as the growth curve for events like these? Is it all driven by the market place?

Kenn Roberts — These events evolve. We sometimes think about going back to the old days, when we could do something at a smaller venue like Pier 6 and have someone like the Oak Ridge Boys. Like you, I'm especially fond of that "Thank God for Kids" concert they gave several years ago. We made a little less money then we do today but we enjoyed it a little more and it was certainly less stressful than these big venue events. There is a lot to be said for a smaller situation with a higher price ticket. We did a show in Aspen this year which was a tribute to John Denver at the Weaver Opera House and it was just a delight to be in such a cozy venue. Of course all that thinking changes when we sign a major performer like Randy Travis. Then we are locked into the thrill of new mountains to climb. It seems we also evolve with the event itself.

Jim Hollan — Final thoughts?

Kenn Roberts — You know, off the record, I'm sorry you're writing this book because it seems too many people are trying to get in the game. I'm fearful it will ruin it for everybody. It won't, but the field is a lot tighter these days. On the other hand I'm glad that an accurate picture can be developed for people who don't really know what's involved. If you ask me to look to the future, I would point out that this concert business is really controlled by the major promoters and it's getting more difficult for small promoters to operate. Big promoters operate at an entirely different level. They are tough business people. I'm not saying they aren't nice people, but they are in this business seven days a week and they are not operating in the same way we are. When we moved to bigger venues we found ourselves bidding, side by side, with the big promoters and we simply don't have the clout that they do. They control more and more of the market and I believe it will be harder to put on concerts like ours over time.

McShane Glover is the president of Noteworthy Productions. She is a theatrical agent in addition to a production specialist and she has been involved in staging everything from major city arts festivals and parades to concerts featuring some of America's top performers. She was involved in the first nine Cystic Fibrosis concerts and helped move that event from a small local festival to an annual concert featuring superstars like Kenny Rogers. We've shared a number of concerts from small start-up local events in tiny halls to city wide festivals to The Ray Charles Concert featured in this book. She is a concert jack of all trades, able to step in at any level of production from promotion to booking but she is particularly a specialist in the myriad intricacies of stage management and production. Her point of view comes from a slightly different perspective.

Jim Hollan — Let me ask you to toss out some advice for those non profits considering an annual concert as a fund-raising event.

McShane Glover — The first thing that you need to know is what you have and where you're going with it. In other words you need to know what your resources are and set some kind of goal, otherwise, you can endlessly discuss what you *might* be doing. The whole entertainment industry is so fascinating that committees often get together and talk about fun things when they need to focus on some concrete elements like how much money they actually have available to work with. The answer to that question makes a whole batch of other decisions for you. For example, what venues and performers are available in that price range. From the base figure, you ask yourself what other dollars might we raise, then you balance the potential and available dollars as you try to come up with a budget.

You set a goal based on that budget. For example, do you want to just make your money back and settle for a lot of positive publicity? Perhaps you want to make a profit of $50,000 above your costs. I think people need to strive for something and goals help shape the framework of an event, otherwise, you just sort of limp along doing nothing.

Jim Hollan — If a local non profit is committed to trying a concert as a fund raiser and they have the funds to start small or actually start with a larger venue right off the bat, what would you advise them to do?

McShane Glover — My two cents is to invest as much as possible. In other words if you have $50,000 to invest, try to make the most of it. Create a memorable event. If you have an "in" with a venue that allows you to knock five grand off the price then great, but don't go to a venue that isn't quite right in order to knock five grand off the price. I guess what I'm saying is that you want to use your money wisely, but if you want to present a high ticket event it is going to cost. People don't pay a lot of money for an okay event, they pay a lot of money for a great event.

Interestingly enough, I find that many event sponsors undervalue their VIP events. It is a big mistake and hard to rectify later. It is also very difficult to move the VIP price up when you've started low. Part of the problem is that some committees fail to think big. They become terrified of their own event. You can't let it intimidate you because it has great potential. I will add that it's okay to be nervous and worried but the committee cannot allow that nervousness to get out of the committee room. Your public image must always be "This is a great event and everyone will love it." You must be enthusiastic. You must be cheerleaders. All the while, you must also do your homework.

Jim Hollan — What do you mean by that?

McShane Glover — Reading the newspaper. Watching what other people are doing. Checking to see if other events are booked for your potential dates. What are their ticket prices? How are they setting up their ads? Picking up the phone after an event and calling the folks who did it to find out how things went. Calling around to check on the costs of different venues. It's all common sense research and it's all stuff you would do if you were planning on spending this kind of money to renovate your house. You must use some of the trades to answer technical questions like how to locate agents for performers. You need to get *Pollstar* or *Cavalcade of Acts and Attractions.* If the organization doesn't know about these basics then they need to find someone like me to get them pointed in the right direction.

Jim Hollan — Where do they find someone like you?

McShane Glover — You start calling people who've just done shows that you've read about in the paper. As you call around, you'll start to hear some names repeated. Call the venues and ask for the names of any producers they can recommend or not recommend. It's not really rocket science, it's common sense backed up with hard work and persistence.

Jim Hollan — I've focused on the VIP reception and meet and greet as events within the event. How do you use these events and how important are they?

McShane Glover — I think the meet and greet fits well into the high ticket item series. If you are looking for big sponsors then you are going to have to treat them very well before, during and after the event. Part of what they are paying for is the chance to press the flesh of the performer. The meet and greet is an absolute necessity for your client and I certainly recognize the need to do it. From a production point of view it's an annoyance. Most performers recognize the need for it but they really don't want to do it. Some performers don't give you a lot of latitude so make sure you negotiate it with management before you sign the contract. You can't always cover all your bases and you will find that some details are floating right up to the moment the meet and greet happens. I also think that a lot of people starting out try to reinvent the wheel. They do one concert a year and they want the program to fit into their preconceived notion of a "concert." Much of the time they would be better off going to the performer's representation and asking what their format is. The performer probably puts on over 250 shows a year and they are likely to have a format already laid out. If you are flexible your needs can fit into their format. Ask. It's not true in all cases, but it does fit in from time to time and life is a whole lot simpler when it does.

Jim Hollan — Talk about the details of planning a bit.

McShane Glover — Groups don't recognize the level at which they have to control things. Control parking. Control security. Control crowds. Make sure you have a solid, reliable team in place the day of the event. Every member should be clear as to their role. Also, the team needs a way to communicate in a larger venue. People really do try to sneak backstage. Venues and performer management will raise the issue of security and it must be addressed. I've run into very dangerous situations trying to move people back for a meet and greet when large stage equipment was being rapidly moved up and down a hallway they had to cross. It wasn't until we had those people backstage and I had to grab a kid about to get run down by a hand truck filled with lights that I realized how dangerous it was. It was just a tiny detail and it could have been a disaster. I thought I'd done it all and here was a new piece that we overlooked. I can tell you that it is always on my check list now. In fact I walk through every traffic pattern before I put it down on paper. You must manage details.

Sometimes you catch on an idea and it seems like a good idea at first but then it starts to go wrong. For example you might have a special presentation during your reception that requires more and more time to make work. There is a tendency to just soldier on rather than re-assess the value of the presentation. There is a difference between persistence and beating your head against the wall and it's a wise person who knows it. If you are starting to feel a certain element is becoming a major struggle and you're swimming up stream you may need to readjust and say this is not as important as I think it is.

Jim Hollan — What works and what's important?

McShane Glover — I remember the Spring Festival we put on for Annapolis. It was very successful and drew over 65,000 people and it basically all came about because we had some very enthusiastic people involved. I think that is a key to successful events. You need some enthusiasm, some "Gosh, isn't this wonderful." I think if there is going to be magic it happens because you have a performer who is open to helping it happen.

Jim Hollan — What do you mean? Give me an example.

McShane Glover — Alabama. They are a real family unit. They have cousins in the office, an aunt driving a truck and an uncle handling merchandise. That sort of community approach to performing carries through in everything. Everyone associated with that show is fully professional but also downright friendly. They are clear about what they want and they are very knowledgeable, but on top of that the people themselves simply went out of their way to be nice. They made the event more than a business transaction. It comes through in their performance. Everyone is working for a great show. That's the way it is when it's right. A team of people coming together with a common goal of creating a great show. It's magic.

My basic advice to the person getting started in the concert process is to focus on the details, read the riders to contracts, ask whom you should talk to about key issues such as lighting or promotion or housing details. Ask questions. Contracts are usually written for worst case scenarios and can contain all sorts of extras not needed. I've called to find out if a rug was mandatory for a stage set up in a concert hall and was told "Oh, no. We just write that in for open-air stages. We don't need that for this show." Confirm conversations afterward in writing so everyone is clear.

My job is to keep expenses down and put on a good show without jeopardizing the quality of the show. If we can get by with 10 stage hands instead of the 14 they call for, that can save us a ton of money, but I don't want to take it down to eight if that means we are going to do a bad show. Gosh, what a concept: as always, communication is the key!

Jim Hollan — You've done everything from small concerts to very large ones. What are some of the differences and challenges?

McShane Glover — Moving up to very large concerts I had to go back and do a lot of research. I'd developed good relationships with the IATSE (International Alliance of Theatrical and Stage Employees) stage hands over the years and that really paid off. I was faced with things I'd never done before like "flying the sound." Suddenly I had to think about riggers and climbers and a forklift. If I hadn't been working as a team with the people who do this every-day, I might not have been able to do the job. Instead, the people in the arena were willing to educate me since we had worked togeth-er on other, smaller events. Overall, I can't emphasize enough how supportive our local #19 have been — real pros and I respect them for that. Interestingly enough, larger venues are often easier from the production end since you deal exclusively with professionals who do this everyday.

When you step down to smaller venues, local halls that seat many hundreds not many thousands, you are often dealing with amateurs. Many of them are very knowledgeable but I ask a lot more questions. I expect to do a lot more myself. I assume that I am going to have to take care of more details. I find it is harder to con-tact people in smaller venues. When I call the arena there is some-one there every day, it's a business. When I call a smaller venue I may get an answering machine that is cleared once a week.

Regardless of the size, you need a visionary somewhere and you need a visionary who is very high energy. If you have a disin-terested or disconnected board of directors backing you up, then go for the little concert since you won't have the promotional support you need for big concert success. If you have a team willing to do their part to make your event a success, then I believe you should stretch and go for the bigger event. I believe that good organizations grow by stretching. Enthusiasm is contagious. This whole thing is entertainment! This is show business! When you do it right it's an easy sell.

P. Michael Meyerstein is the Director of Development and Com-munications for Beth Tfiloh. He is also a Certified Fund Raising Executive, a member of that small community of fund-raising pro-fessionals who have established their credentials by years of experi-ence as well as years of specialized education in all aspects of fund raising. Michael also has his own consulting firm, the Aleph Group, Inc. In addition to running traditional campaigns, he also secures celebrity performances so that organizations can replicate his event. His expertise is evidenced by his ability to put his own unique spin on the standard concert event we have just described. Michael has obtained extraordinary results by adjusting a few key principles and I believe he perfectly illustrates that success comes not from rigid imitation but from the ability to apply basic principles to your unique needs, adjusting when appropriate. I'm going to ask him to talk about his annual event at Beth Tfiloh and you should quickly see how he has adjusted some basics so that his event now has a unique life of its own.

Jim Hollan — To this point in my book I've discussed traditional concerts that charge standard ticket prices which fundamentally cover the costs of the concert. Profits are made on a growing base of sponsor dollars. I also suggest that big names come with big venues. You bring big names to a small venue, have a hefty ticket price and your event is extraordinarily successful year after year. Would you describe your event for our readers, touching in particular on the size of your venue and your ticket pricing?

Michael Meyerstein — Our venue is approximately 1,500 seats and we fill it. This past June, when we brought in Bill Cosby, we actually put in another 150 chairs and set up a live video feed to another part of the building. Our tickets are $175, $100 and $75.The reason we charge what we do is that our market allows it. Bringing in a high-caliber performer does allow you to charge more. I quickly point out to my clients in my consulting business, however, that people give to people more than they give to causes. The reason someone is willing to spend $175 per ticket to see Cosby or Art Garfunkel or Itzhak Perlman is because someone has asked them to come with them or asked them to buy the ticket. Yes, we get people who see the invitation and order a ticket, but I would say that our higher-end tickets are sold because someone has asked the ticket buyer to buy.

Jim Hollan — What kind of dollars are you generating in a venue that size?

Michael Meyerstein — To give a little history to this, when I started with the organization about seven years ago, they were netting approximately $50,000 and were filling about a 1,000 seats. This past June our net from the event was $300,000 on a gross of approximately $465,000.

Jim Hollan — Holy Cow! That's amazing, Michael. That's an extraordinary income for a venue that small. What a success.

Michael Meyerstein — Thank you for the accolades, but we raise the bar after every success, and right now I'm chewing my fingernails. This year's event is six months away and I'm four months behind in getting a chairman! People are turning us down because the event has become too successful and too daunting and, I think, too intimidating. People are reluctant to step to the plate because they don't want to fail. We are suddenly becoming victims of our own success.

Jim Hollan — Tell me a bit about your corporate sponsorships.

Michael Meyerstein — That is a key to our financial success over the years. When I started there were six businesses that gave us money over and above the ticket prices, and that was because two board members approached their vendors to give a few thousand dollars. At that time the revenue was all of $35,000. This past June, it hit $325,000 coming from 200 businesses. It has grown substantially, and I would say that we still have plenty of room for growth. It just takes a lot of perseverance and determination to get your committee members to open up their Rolodexes and contact their prospects.

Jim Hollan — Do you look at this event primarily for the money raised or do you look beyond that?

Michael Meyerstein — Obviously it's done for the dollars, but equally important, we see this as a friend raiser. It's a school sponsored event and we pull into the audience people who represent a cross section of the community. For the past few years we've begun the event with a six or seven-minute video that profiles lots of smiling faces of children and activities. In a way it's not just PR, but an admissions recruitment vehicle. This year we had one of the children present Bill Cosby with a special award and it was a very effective moment. All 1,500 program books had a hand written 4x6 card which is written by our students. Depending on their ability to write, the child might write a note that says "Dear Guest, Thank you for coming tonight. We appreciate your support and we thank you for thinking of us." For our younger grades, it might be some chicken scratch with a picture. Still, it is very effective and it adds a personal touch.

Jim Hollan — I know that you had a special reception with kids and Bill Cosby. Would you tell me a little about that?

Michael Meyerstein — In order for a child to be able to attend, a ticket had to be purchased for that child. By virtue of that purchase the child was eligible to come to the pre-event meeting with Cosby. We had well over 100 kids present of all ages. When we structured the reception with Cosby's people, it was left very fluid. He would allow children to come up and ask him questions and he would give his very clever answers. I must say that it worked beautifully and it lasted approximately 45 minutes.

Jim Hollan — Wow, that's a lovely variation. Do you use any other VIP reception or meet and greet at your event?

Michael Meyerstein — Oh yes. Cosby did not want to do an after-show event because he wanted to catch a plane. So we created a special cocktail reception before the concert to which we invited only our major corporate sponsors. They had a chance to have their photo taken with Cosby. We always have special receptions at our events.

Jim Hollan — Off the top of your head, Michael, could you share some advice for someone thinking of a start-up event like yours?

Michael Meyerstein — I'll tell you what I tell my clients. If an organization is starting out with a celebrity event, I urge conservatism. Because it's a first time effort, I tell them to exaggerate the expenses, underestimate the income, and go for a level of talent below which they ideally would like, so that they are not subject to a lot of risk and exposure. In order for them to determine how much talent they can afford, I tell them to back into that number. Essentially they should create a budget. Plug into that budget anticipated income, anticipated expenses as well as what the minimum dollar amount is that they need to net from the event. After they subtract out expenses from income they will know how much money is left for the performer. They can then go shopping for a performer based on that number. That is a very conservative way of doing it, but I get to sleep better at night and so does the client. Once they have a data base of satisfied customers for next year, they can raise the prices a little, secure a couple more corporate sponsors, to give them a little more latitude to attract a bigger name. Everyone must walk before they can run.

So now you've heard from three experts in the field, all very accomplished, all well respected and all very successful, yet, each with unique differences as to the way they stage an event like this. It is equally clear that they all share a basic structural similarity when it comes to presenting such an event. For all of them it is about much more than money. They focus on all the details that make an event special, recognizing that their key constituency over time is the satisfied customer. They strive to put on an event that will be first rate with the belief that people will keep coming back for more. They all grow the event so that it fits the unique character of their organization.

Chapter 15
Final Thoughts

The first concert is always the most difficult one to stage since almost everything you do is guesswork. You have no real experience on which to base your assumptions other than similar events in your area. Everything we've talked about to this point is guesswork the first time out; however, all of that changes after the first one is over. From that point on you know what worked and what didn't. You have a base on which you can build year after year. You can fix those things that don't work well and you can improve those things that can use improving as you fine tune your event. Run properly, you actually get to the point where your net income increases annually for the first few years as the amount of work and planning actually decreases. Several years out, you should have an event that starts to level off with a fairly predictable income and a fairly predictable cost. The concert should not only be a fund raiser, it should also be a friend raiser, an annual chance for your supporters to come together in celebration of a great cause. Run properly as a sophisticated and stylish event, you won't have to ask them to bring their associates, they will do so on their own and you will have the opportunity to develop these "friends of friends" into your friends.

Going back to our original planning for the Ray Charles concert it was our goal to raise between $25,000 and $50,000 in net profit the first year out against income of approximately $100,000 as we established a first-year event. In other words our net profit would be approximately 25% to 50% for our first-year event. The fact is that we raised just over $100,000 and our net profit was just over $30,000. We came in exactly as predicted but we did not have a sell out at the theatre. Although the crowd was very respectable, we had 700 seats left over. Since all the costs were already covered, every one of those ticket sales would have been pure profit! A sell out would have pushed our net profit right up to the $50,000 level. The Maryland School for the Blind made a quantum leap in public recognition, press coverage and new friend making. We were delighted with these first-year results.

It was our belief that we could refine the second-year concert, keep expenses about the same and slightly increase our income and net profit. We believe that we can reduce the cost of certain items like printing, by having more services donated; furthermore, we believe that our sponsor dollars will increase slightly and our very profitable VIP ticket buyers will increase in number. A rough guess for Year 2 has projected income at $125,000 with expenses the same or slightly less than Year 1. We believe net profit will be in the $50,000 to $75,000 range which means our net income moves up to a more respectable 40% to 60% of total income by the second year as we grow our event.

In Year 3 we expect our event to have a place in the community and a solid base of supporters as we continue growing. In Year 3 we anticipate our expenses to be about the same as Year 2 or slightly higher and we expect ticket prices also to stay about the same. If you remember our discussions about sponsors back in Chapter 4, we decided to charge about half the going rate for similar sponsorships in our area for the first two years out. Since our event will be established by Year 3, we believe that we can move our sponsor levels up and we anticipate keeping most of our sponsors and adding one or two replacements for those that might drop out. We believe our sponsor dollars will double over Year 2. We predict net income in Year 3 to approach $175,000 with net profit moving to $100,000 to $125,000. The net profit will now be in the much more acceptable 57% to 71% range. Our three-year goal is to have an event that realizes an annual net profit of $100,000 while developing a positive public image and giving new visibility to our organization.

Let's say we accomplish that goal. Then what? What do we do next? The fact is that we've come full circle. We have accomplished our goal and we can keep this concert as an annual event in our arsenal of fund-raising/friend-raising tools. We must recognize that this event goes far beyond the dollars raised directly from the concert as a development tool for our organization. It is a chance for us to involve potential new supporters for our cause. It is a chance to network in a fun environment with our current supporters. It is an opportunity to get our name in front of the public in a positive way every year. It is an opportunity to network with media, political and celebrity personalities who may become more involved with our cause. It is an opportunity to get our corporate dollar sponsors involved as corporate "people" sponsors. It is an opportunity to develop new "first name" relationships with new friends. In the process we raise at least $100,000 of new funds every year.

We come now to a crossroad where we have a few choices. We can leave this concert where it is and keep it as an annual event we know and understand. If we want to grow another event we can focus on something totally different for a different time of the year. Maybe a celebrity golf tournament or race for a cure or whatever suits your fancy. If we are a state wide organization we may want to run a similar event in a very distant part of the state at a very different time of the year, but we must not compete with our own event. It really makes no sense to borrow from Peter to pay Peter. We may decide that one special event is enough and we may focus our energies on maximizing the return from this event. Remember the success Mike Meyerstein has with only 1,500 seats? Netting over $300,000 with a venue that size is a worthy goal for any organization.

We may have this concert as one key element in a mix of many different kinds of events that are held year-round. I'm not making these scenarios up, I'm listing what organizations actually do. Non profits have their own flavor and you must do what works best for you and your resources.

The other possibility for your successful concert is to keep growing . Like the successful Cystic Fibrosis concert series listed in Chapter 1, you can start small and keep moving up the ladder until you have an event than generates hundreds of thousands of dollars in profits while accomplishing all of your other development and friend-making goals. Before making that decision, however, realize that you will have a lot more work in store for your team as you move from venue to venue. It's a great opportunity, but also an ongoing risk as you move up that ladder. The size and logistics involved will require a year-long planning staff and the event will require constant attention. I'm not arguing against that possibility. In fact, some organizations hire a part time, year-long staff person to man the annual desk for a major event. Their work is minimal for six months, busy for three months and totally chaotic for the final three months leading up to the event. My point is that you must stop and evaluate your goals at each new step on the ladder.

Which way is the best way? Whichever one suits you, your organization and your team. Thousands of "me too" events will eventually condemn us all to failure but properly designed events will always help define, showcase and grow an organization. Concerts are *one* of the many tools in the professional fund-raising tool box. I'm not suggesting that you have a concert for your organization, nor am I suggesting that you not have one. My goal was to eliminate the silly "concerts and special events are a waste of time" nonsense that I've heard from people who should know better. I set out to walk you through a real concert, recognizing full well that one can only paint a picture in time. I hope that you now have a much better sense as to how concerts work. I hope that you can take that knowledge and see how it fits in with the needs of your organization. I hope you have a better understanding as to how this tool works and how it may or may not fit in with your needs and the needs of your organization. You don't ever need to stage a concert to be an effective fund raiser, but I think it speaks well for you that you at least know how they work. I hope this book helped.

Bibliography

Arledge, R., and D. Friedman. *Dynamic Fund Raising Projects* (Chicago: Precept Press, Inc., 1992).

Aspen's Guide to 60 Successful Special Events: How to Plan, Organize and Conduct Outstanding Fund Raisers (Gaithersburg, MD: Aspen Publishers, Inc., 1996).

Ernst & Young. *The Complete Guide to Special Event Management: Business Insights, Financial Advice and Strategies* (New York: John Wiley & Sons, 1992).

Goldblatt, J. *Special Events: Best Practices in Modern Event Management* (New York: Van Nostrand Reinhold, 1996).

Greenfield, J. *Fund-Raising: Evaluating and Managing the Fund Development Process* (New York: John Wiley & Sons, 1991).

Harris, A. *Raising Money and Cultivating Donors Through Special Events* (Washington, DC: Council for Advancement and Support of Education, 1991).

Kaitcer, C. *Raising Big Bucks Through Pledge-Based Special Events: How to Plan Successful Walks and Bike Tours* (Chicago: Bonus Books, 1996).

Levy, B., and B. Marion. *Successful Special Events: Planning, Hosting, and Evaluating* (Gaithersburg, MD: Aspen Publishers, Inc. 1997).

Smith, Bucklin and Associates. *The Complete Guide to Nonprofit Management* (New York: John Wiley & Sons, 1994).

Index